Tortoises and Turtles

Vincenzo Ferri

Tortoises
and Turtles

A FIREFLY BOOK

Published by Firefly Books
Ltd. 2002

Copyright © 1999 Arnoldo
Mondadori Editore S.P.A.
English translation © Arnoldo
Mondadori Editore S.p.A.
All rights reserved.

First Printing 2002

**Publisher Cataloging-in-
Publication Data (U.S.)**

Ferri, Vincenzo.
 Turtles and tortoises : a
Firefly guide / Vincenzo
Ferri. -- 1st ed.
[256] p. : col. photos. ; cm.
Includes bibliographical
references and index.
Summary: A comprehensive
guide to turtles and tortoises
including habitat,
dimensions, biology and
behavior.
ISBN 1-55209-631-9 (pbk.)
1. Turtles. 2. Sea turtles.
I. Title.
597.92 21 CIP
QL666.C5.F47 2002

**National Library of Canada
Cataloguing in Publication
Data**

Ferri, Vincenzo
 Turtles and tortoises : a
Firefly guide

Translated from the original
Italian 1999 ed., Tutto
tartarughe e testuggini,
by Anna Bennett.
Includes bibliographical
references and index.
ISBN 1-55209-631-9

 1. Turtles. I. Bennett,
Anna II. Title.

QL666.C5F4713 2002 597.92
C2001-902621-8

Published in Canada
in 2002 by
Firefly Books Ltd.
3680 Victoria Park Avenue
Willowdale, Ontario M2H 3K1

Published in the U.S.
in 2002 by
Firefly Books (U.S.) Inc.
P.O. Box 1338,
Ellicott Station
Buffalo, New York 14205

English text edited by
Charlotte DuChene

Front cover photograph ©
Marc C. Chamberlain, M.D./
DRK PHOTO

Printed in Spain
D.L.TO: 2011-2001

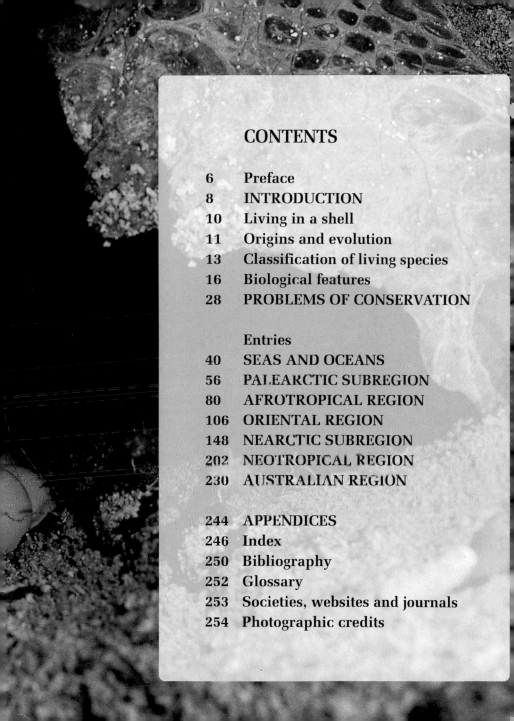

CONTENTS

Scholars have long been fascinated by turtles and tortoises. This may be due to their odd appearance or possibly because some experts believe them to be the ancestors of the mammals. In any event, these reptiles have always played an important role both in the collective imagination and in scientific circles. It was in 1831 that J. E. Gray made the first comprehensive study of the Chelonia, listing all the world's species known at that time. As often happens, the publication of this book, excellent for its period, stimulated a considerable growth in research. This produced a mass of descriptions of new species, which soon rendered Gray's book obsolete, despite the supplements that the author hastened to add (Gray 1855, 1870, 1872, etc.).

This was more or less the fate of ensuing volumes on the subject, and little changed in this sense until the middle of the 20th century. The book by Wermuth and Mertens (1961) was followed by those of Pritchard (1967, 1979) and finally by that of Ernst and Barbour (1989). These dealt, for the most part, with species that had already been classified, but during the second half of the century, zoologists broadened their scope and set off in new directions. It is impossible to list here the enormous mass of specialized literature devoted to the biology and physiognomy of this group of animals, for which we must turn to the books by Swingland (1989). Of those that sum up the principal aspects of research on the Chelonia, I will therefore limit myself to the fine book by Harless and Morlock (1989).

Around the mid-20th century, the concept of biological conservation began to take shape. Major developments in technology, the increase in world population and the all too evident impoverishment of nonrenewable resources contributed to the conviction that it was now high time to do something to prevent the natural environment from being transformed to such an extent that it would no longer be able to support most of the existing animal and plant species. Thus, from the 1950s, students of natural history tended in the main to envisage animals as subjects to catalog, enumerate and enrich museum collections. Subsequently, many students focused their scientific activities on the problem of biological conservation. Turtles, once again, were the first reptiles to evoke this special concern. The Convention on International Trade in Endangered Species (CITES), covering animals and plants, listed in Appendix I some 23 species for which virtually all forms of commerce at the international level were prohibited. For many others, especially in Europe, trading was strictly regulated. Investigation was facilitated by the fact that these reptiles were slow-moving creatures, fairly easy to locate and, above all, strictly linked to their natural surroundings or at least still little affected by human interference.

Yet the threat was there. The thick, heavy carapace, which had enabled them to protect themselves against predatory attacks of all kinds from the end of the Triassic to the present day, no longer seemed to offer them such a great advantage in an environment where man, more than ever, predominated. The *1996 IUCN Red List of Threatened Animals* (Baillie and Groombridge) listed some 96 species at risk of extinction, about one-third of all those known. It is now recognized that protection of an animal species entails more than merely trying to check the flow of commerce for whatever ultimate purpose. Indeed, what is vitally important is to try to preserve their natural habitat. Various books in recent years have confronted this problem in detail (Bjorndal, 1981, Ballasina, 1995). As relates to many other fields of inquiry, however, the problem is now one of synthesis. On the one hand, as knowledge increases and data accumulate, the volume of scientific literature grows in proportion; on the other hand, by virtue of this very fact, available information risks becoming so vast as to be almost inaccessible.

It is in this context that Vincenzo Ferri's book must be seen. Not only does it provide photographs of more than two-thirds of the known species of turtles and tortoises, but it facilitates identification of these and the rest through individual entries. It also comprehensively describes the physical, biological and zoological characteristics of the various species and provides a mass of information on the current state of conservation that they enjoy, as well as underlining the threats and dangers to which they are increasingly exposed. This book will be of value to ordinary readers and particularly to those concerned with the interests of these astonishing reptiles—concerned about protecting them from clandestine traffic or ready to lend support to programs designed to preserve their habitats and prevent already sparse populations from vanishing. Needless to say, I share the hopes of all who feel deeply about the survival of these amazing animals, and it is in this spirit that I commend this book and wish it deserved success.

Emilio Balletto
President of the Italian Herpetological
Society, Department of Animal and
Human Biology, University of Turin

INTRODUCTION

Notes for ease of reference

The individual page entries describe the majority of living species and subspecies of turtles and tortoises according to the latest information concerning fauna and taxonomy. They have been subdivided according to the biogeographical regions of current distribution and origin, with reference to the work of Zunino and Zullini (1995). Thus there are illustrations—with one or more examples—of more than 170 species of Chelonia, including a number of extremely localized, rare or recently discovered species. For certain species, however, which are little known or living in surroundings that are difficult to access, it has not been possible to find photographs taken in nature; those of special interest or importance from the conservation viewpoint have nevertheless been illustrated by color drawings. It is the author's aim to continue researching such material with a view to making future editions of this book more comprehensive.

In the case of all the species considered, the following data are given: geographical distribution, habitat, principal characteristics (morphological and biological) and the present situation in light of national regulations and programs of protection and conservation. Each region or subregion is introduced by a general overview

in which the endemic families and genera are noted. In the numbered entries for individual species, a map illustrates the known distribution. For each family of Chelonia, there is a boxed sequential list of features for identifying the genera in which the existing species are grouped; reference is made only to those morphological features which are evident in the live animal (based on the identification tables of Ernst and Barbour, 1989, and the CITES checklists, 1995).

The tables in the present book provide pointers to genus determination by offering two alternatives, each giving a direction to further information. The index of chelonian species at the end of the book lists, by family, all the species (and to some extent the subspecies) previously described or systematically identified (on the basis of the Turtle, Tuatara and Crocodile Checklist by F. Wayne King and R. L. Burke, 1997, and contributions published in the scientific journal Chelonian Conservation and Biology by Behler, Pritchard and Rhodin, 1996–98). The page numbers in the index refer to the individual entry or specific mention of that species or subspecies in the book.

LIVING WITH A SHELL

It may appear presumptuous to try to describe the highly diversified world of turtles and tortoises in a single book: indeed, even specialists have modestly admitted that we still know all too little about these animals and that discoveries continue to surface with such rapidity that it is difficult even to count the number of official-

ly recognized species. What this book aims to achieve is to discuss and illustrate the physical, biological and behavioral characteristics of the majority of known species in the context of their present-day environment.

The general term "chelonian" will refer to the group in its entirety; so, too, will the name "turtle." Strictly speaking, however, a turtle is an aquatic species, whereas the term "tortoise" is applicable to terrestrial species.

These creatures are among the most successful of all animal groups in that they have retained their unusual body structure almost without modification since the distant Triassic era, some 200 million years ago. This characteristic anatomical form represents one of the most interesting adaptations in the world of vertebrates, and the robust "shell" that covers the body is without doubt the secret of their successful evolution. Many orders of reptiles developed over an extremely long period only to disappear around 65 million years ago, probably as a result of geological and climatic upheavals following the breakup of the original single continental platform (Pangea) into the present-day continents. The most plausible explanation of the disaster is that because the thousands of animals then living on Earth were by that time so highly specialized in their lifestyles, they were incapable of adapting to new environmental conditions. The striking anatomical and biological uniformity of the Chelonia

Previous spread, an adult and young of the rarest species of land tortoise, Geochelone yniphora. *Above, the head of* Chelonia mydas.

and their opportunist methods of food gathering (with the development of a portable shell, they ceased to be predators and, in the main, made the transition to a vegetarian or omnivorous diet) were surely contributory factors toward their survival.

Left, Caretta caretta; *above, adult of* Rhinoclemmys pulcherrima.

ORIGIN AND EVOLUTION

The general body structure of a turtle is unmistakable, enclosed as it usually is within a strong shell. However, it is not widely realized that it is a reptile and, moreover, that it belongs to one of the few surviving orders of these vertebrates. Indeed, the order of Testudines (Batsh, 1788) or Chelonia is believed to be the oldest of all: the earliest fossil evidence dates back to the Permian period, about 280 million years ago. Reptiles as a group have had an astonishing evolution, beginning in the Carboniferous period, when a group of primitive amphibians abandoned the water and gradually colonized the surrounding areas of land. There is no certainty as to why this happened. The

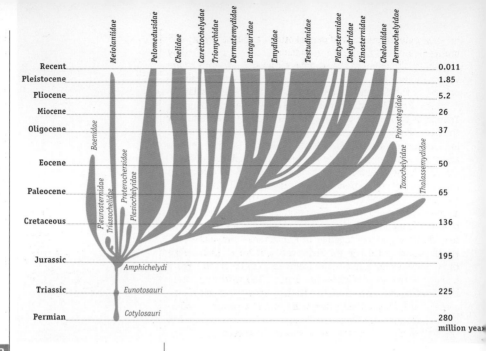

	Meiolaniidae		Pelomedusidae	Chelidae	Carettochelydae	Trionychidae	Dermatemydidae	Bataguridae	Emydidae		Testudinidae	Platysternidae	Chelydridae	Kinosternidae	Cheloniidae	Dermochelyidae
Recent																	0.011
Pleistocene																	1.85
Pliocene																	5.2
Miocene																	26
Oligocene																	37
Eocene																	50
Paleocene																	65
Cretaceous																	136
Jurassic																	195
Triassic																	225
Permian																	280

Baenidae *Pleurosternidae* *Triassochelidae* *Proterochersidae* *Plesiochelyidae* *Protostegidae* *Toxochelyidae* *Thalassemyidae*

Amphichelydi

Eunotosauri

Cotylosauri

million years

12

Diagram: one interpretation of the phylogenesis of the Chelonia based on geographical eras.

Above, free swimming action of a very young Chelonia mydas.

coastal ponds and lakes must have by then been very crowded in comparison with the dry land and presented greater dangers and fewer food opportunities. Complete liberation from the water was fully achieved with the development of the amniote egg, the first egg to have a hard shell. Inside the shell, the developing embryo is encased in a fluid-filled cavity comprising three membranes: the amnion, the allantois and the chorion. This system of embryonic development, fundamental in protecting the embryo from dehydration, constituted an important step toward the so-called Amniota (reptiles, birds and mammals) becoming future rulers of the Earth.

The first true land vertebrates were known as cotylosaurs (Cotylosauria)—reptiles that flourished and developed in the late Paleozoic. Their appearance was very archaic, their movements still notably awkward. It is almost certainly from this original stock that the ancestors of the chelonians evolved, although forming a side branch. Fossil examples of these earliest terrestrial creatures are rare; to find fossils known to represent the first evolutionary stage of the turtles, we must therefore look back to the Permian. These are tiny skeletons of eunotosaurs (*Eunotosaurus africanus*), discovered in South Africa. Already present, in fact, is a defensive dorsal armor casing comparable to that of the chelonians (composed of a series

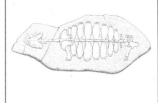

of bony nodules, probably of dermal origin, and a flattening and broadening of the ribs); on the abdomen, not yet protected by a plastron, the bones of the scapular girdle and the sternum are very broad and flat. Testimony to these cotylosaurian origins is offered by the presence of teeth in the jaw and in the palate.

It was about 200 million years ago, however, during the upper Triassic in present-day Germany, that the first true ancestors of the chelonians appeared. These left fossil forms similar to the Cheloniidae and Dermatemydidae, families that still survive, with an arrangement of bony plates on the carapace and plastron. Examination of these same fossils (for example, *Triassochelys dux*) shows the anatomical connection with the eunotosaurs; in their palate, too, a series of small teeth may be observed. The Triassochelidae, as they were named, had a widespread distribution, with dozens of forms living on land (the most primitive), in ponds and in the sea. They are grouped together in the suborder Amphichelydia, which became extinct in the Pleistocene but from which sprang the two still extant suborders of Pleurodira and Cryptodira. Fossil remains of the Amphichelidae are divided into three superfamilies: Proganochelyidea (from the Triassic, with the species *Triassochelys dux*, *Proganochelys quenstedti* and *Proterochersus robusta*), Pleurosternoidea (from the Jurassic to the Cretaceous) and finally Baenoidea (from the Cretaceous to the Eocene).

CLASSIFICATION OF LIVING SPECIES

The Chelonia are amniotic vertebrates, in that they are born from a hard-shelled egg containing three characteristic membranes: the *amnion* (which surrounds the embryo, forming the amniotic sac, a liquid-filled cavity in which it develops), the *chorion* (a protective membrane) and the *allantois*, which allows gaseous exchanges and the storage of toxic metabolic secretions. Classification of the Amniota was based until recent years on the type and number of temporal openings in the skull: Anapsid (without temporal fossae), Diapsid (two pairs of fossae), Parapsid (with the two upper fossae only) and Synapsid (with the two lower fossae only).

All primitive vertebrates, from the crossopterigians to the cotylosaurs, had the skeleton of the head formed by a bony roof entirely of dermal origin, slightly broken by the apertures for the external nostrils, the orbits and the parietal foramen. In contrast to the bones of other amniotes, there appeared a lateral slit, the temporal fossae, which facilitated the attachment and development of the temporal muscles. Recent taxonomic studies have shown that the evolutionary lineage of the Chelonia is very different from that of other reptiles.

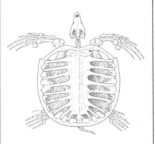

From top to bottom: fossil remains of Eunotosaurus africanus, Triassochelys dux *and* Archelon ischyros.

Identifying the species of present-day turtles

On the basis of the works of Pritchard (1979), Ernst and Barbour (1989), King and Burke (1997) and the CITES checklists (1985), the following simplified identification table covers the existing families of turtles. The characteristics mentioned are, for the most part, clearly visible on the live animal; some difficulty may arise in the recognition of specimens belonging to the two families of pond turtles, Bataguridae and Emydidae, in which the differences are anatomical. The various families are fully described and illustrated in the individual entries of this book, where they appear in their original biogeographical region or in the region where the present-day species are most widely distributed.

1. Carapace and plastron covered by well-separated scutes or horny plates → 2.
1a. Carapace and plastron covered by skin, without obvious subdivisions into scutes or plates → 13.
2. Front limbs paddle-shaped, without separated digits; one or two claws on each forelimb; intergular scute; members of this family all have a marine habitat → Cheloniidae.
2a. Front limbs columnar with distinct digits, each with four or five claws; more or less evident intergular scute → 3.
3. Neck retracted horizontally into the shell, with a sideways movement; intergular scute; 13 scutes on plastron → 4.
3a. Neck retracted vertically, from front to back; no intergular scute → 5.
4. Carapace never has a nuchal scute; feet adapted for swimming, with heavily webbed hind toes; pond habitat → Pelomedusidae.
4a. Carapace usually has a nuchal scute; limbs adapted for swimming, with well-developed toes; pond habitat → Chelidae.
5. Rigid plastron, lacks movable hinge → 9.
5a. Plastron has one or two movable hinges → 6.
6. Plastron has only one movable hinge → 7.
6a. Plastron has two movable hinges → 8.
7. Front part of the plastron is moved by a hinge situated between the abdominal and pectoral scutes; plastron comprises eight scutes joined to the carapace by a narrow bridge; pond habitat → Kinosternidae.
7a. Front part of the plastron is fixed, but hind part can be moved → genus Pyxis, Testudinidae.
8. Front part of the plastron hinged, both in North and Central American species → genus Terrapene, Emydidae.
8a. Both front and hind parts of plastron hinged: species from eastern Asia → genus Cuora, Bataguridae.
9. One or more inframarginal scutes present on plastron

1. Pelomedusidae
2. Chelidae
3. Kinosternidae
4. Emydidae, genus Terrapene
5. Bataguridae, genus Cuora

14

that separate the pectoral and abdominal scutes from the marginal scutes → 10.

9a. No inframarginal scutes present; pectoral and abdominal scutes in contact with the marginal scutes → 12.

10. Relatively small head; carapace and plastron almost elliptical; jaws denticulate and beak unhooked; short tail; pond habitat → Dermatemydidae.

10a. Large head, hooked beak, small cruciform plastron with rigid bridges or large, elongate plastron with flexible bridges; long, sturdy tail → 11.

11. Small cruciform plastron, rounded anteriorly, bridges rigid; abdominal scutes separated from midline; pond habitat → Chelydridae.

11a. Large plastron, truncated anteriorly, flexible bridges; abdominal scutes in contact with median line; pond habitat → Platysternidae.

12. Elephantine, columnar hind feet with small claws; front limbs covered with osteoderms (bony skin plates); habitat terrestrial→ Testudinidae.

12a. Hind feet not elephantine; toes often somewhat webbed; no osteoderms in forelimbs; habitat typically aquatic → Emydidae (New World, American, except for genus Emys) and Bataguridae (Old World, except for genus Rhinoclemmys).

13. Carapace with five to seven longitudinal projecting ridges; visible cusps on upper jaw; flattened, shovel-like front feet without claws; ocean habitat → Dermochelyidae.

13a. Carapace not ridged and upper jaw without cusps; long neck and much elongated and tubelike snout → 14.

14. Entire marginal border flexible; reduced plastral bones; pond habitat → Trionychidae.

14a. Entire carapace rigid; plastron ossified; pond habitat → Carettochelyidae.

6. Chelydridae
7. Platysternidae
8. Testudinidae
9. Emydidae
10. Bataguridae

From top to bottom: the carapace of Geochelone sulcata and Geochelone carbonaria, and the plastron, with a visible suture, of the Terrapene species.

Drawings, right: the body skeleton of a tortoise seen from the side and from below, without the plastron.

In this newborn individual of the Pelusios species, below, the fontanelle opening of the vitelline membrane is still visible.

BIOLOGICAL FEATURES

Shell

As mentioned, the peculiarity of the Chelonia (except for certain groups) is that the body is protected by a bony shell that comprises a dorsal part (carapace) and a ventral part (plastron), which are either interconnected or, in the majority of species, joined by a more or less bony bridge.

The typical carapace (for example, in the members of the family Testudinidae) has about 50 plates or layers of bony tissue joined together with sutures: 1 nuchal, 9 neural, 1 pygal, 2 suprapygal and two series of pleural. The plastron, however, is composed of 11 bony plates: 2 preplastral, 2 hypoplastral, 2 xiphiplastral and 1 entoplastral. The carapace and plastron are usually covered on the outside with broad horny plates (scutes), typically numbering at least 38 on the carapace and 12 on the plastron, partially overlapping or juxtaposed.

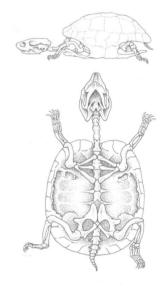

Among the turtles of the families Trionychidae and Dermochelyidae, there are fewer bony plates on the carapace and a skin covering that is particularly solid, almost leathery. In the Dermochelyidae, the covering is strengthened by numerous minute bony plates; in the family Carettochelydae, the carapace is bony, but without the covering of horny plates. Neither the arrangement nor the number of the horny layers, when present, coincide with the underlying bony parts. This discrepancy is the reason for the strength of the shell, capable as it is of protecting either a part of or the entire body of these animals. The number and arrangement of horny plates constitute a useful means of identification.

Duration of life

Turtles and tortoises are considered to be among the longest-living animals, for it has been repeatedly proven that some species (especially among the Testudinidae) may readily live to more than 50 years of age. Indeed, among those bred in captivity, several specimens have reached the age of 100 years. Their average life in the wild, however, based on the evidence of osteo-chronological analysis, indicates a life expectancy of not more than 35 years because of the many threats to which they are exposed (adverse weather conditions, attacks by predators, fires in their habitat and various diseases).

The widespread opinion is that the age of the animals can be "read" by examining the grooves on each horny shield of the carapace. In practice—and only in the case of chelonians of the family Testudinidae that live in temperate or subtropical zones and thus with an alternation of cold-hot, wet-dry seasons—it is possible to calculate the approximate age by counting the visible concentric grooves on one of the horny lateral scutes of the carapace, starting from the central areole. In these species, as growth occurs, each scute progressively expands the marginal surface. This growth is uniform and continues during the phases of activity when the animal is in good physical shape, whereas it is slowed down or blocked during the inactive phases (winter or summer dormancy in the hottest months) or when the animal is debilitated through trauma, disease or lack of food. Each groove, therefore, corresponds to the end of an active period and to the vital stasis (arrest of activity) prior to a new one; the total number, however, does not necessarily coincide with the years of life. With old age, moreover, growth slows down, and the distance between the grooves is reduced, while the continuous wear and tear on the carapace as it rubs against grass and other obstacles interrupts steady development.

Thus the counting of years among the Testudinidae will be more accurate for young individuals with a little-worn carapace. As for the others, tropical Testudinidae and other families in which the structure of the carapace is characterized by smooth horny plates (which in fact are shed periodically with growth) or which do not have a true carapace, we must be satisfied with a rough estimate, based on the known maximum dimensions of adults and on the variable livery typical of newborn, young and adult specimens.

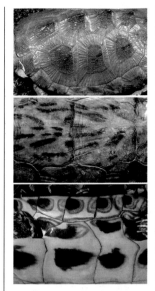

From top to bottom: the horny scutes on the carapace of a Pelomedusidae species, and those on the carapace and plastron of Trachemys scripta elegans.

17

Dimensions

The various families differ considerably in speed of growth, and the full average size is reached at different ages. Certain species of Emydidae grow so rapidly that they reach their maximum dimensions within a mere 4

These small land tortoises (Testudo hermanni), below, are each separated by about one year in age.

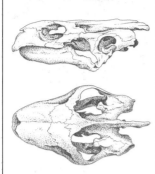

The general appearance of the skull of the Testudinidae.

A comparison between a giant among living tortoises, Geochelone nigra from the Galápagos Islands, center, and a dwarf species, Homopus signatus, from South Africa, below.

to 5 years, while it takes 10 to 12 years for some Testudinidae to attain full size. This coincides with reaching sexual maturity—earlier in small-size species (for example 4 to 5 years in males and 5 to 6 in females of many Emydidae and Bataguridae). As a rule, male Testudinidae are sexually mature at 6 to 8 years, and females at 10 to 12 years; but large specimens of *Geochelone* only begin to reproduce after some 20 years.

In the majority of living species, the maximum length of the carapace is less than 30 cm (12 in); cases of dwarfism or gigantism are exceptional. The extreme records for land-dwelling species are held by the Testudinidae. They boast the smallest forms, such as the South African land tortoise *Homopus signatus*, whose carapace is at most 7 to 10 cm (3–4 in) long, and the largest, such as the giant Aldabra tortoise *Aldabrachelys ele-*

phantina, with a carapace that may grow to a length of 123 cm (4 ft). The size record for living Chelonia, however, goes to a marine species, the leatherback turtle (*Dermochelys coriacea*), with the carapace of certain specimens measuring almost 200 cm (7 ft) and weighing 500 to 600 kg (1,100–1,320 lb). As for extinct species, there were various giants, both from land and sea: first place goes to the representatives of the Protostegidae, marine turtles of the Cretaceous, with a carapace up to almost 3 m (10 ft) long and a weight estimated at over 2,000 kg (4,400 lb). (See the drawing on page 13 of *Archelon ischyros*, from the United States Cretaceous.)

Skeleton and muscles

The skeletal system of the Chelonia contains little cartilage, and a few long bones produce white and red corpuscles (for example, the femur). There is an endoskeleton (internal bones) and an exoskeleton (carapace and plastron); the former is sub-divided into an axial skeleton (skull, vertebrae and ribs) and an appendicular skeleton (bones of limbs and scapular and pelvic girdles). The vertebral column of the Chelonia (comprising 40 to 50 vertebrae of which only the 8 cervical and 25 to 30 cau-dal are independent) is almost entirely connected to the shell by the spinous apophyses of the vertebrae. The ribs, beginning with the 10 thoracic vertebrae, develop along with the costal plates of the carapace, with which they fuse in the course of aging. In the most primitive families, Pleurodirae, some bones of the pelvic girdle are incorporated in the carapace.

The skeleton of the head is primitive in type, called anap-sid, without a true temporal opening; in some families, though, the rear part of the cranial cavity is very small. There are no teeth, but the jaws are covered with a horny layer to form a kind of beak with cutting edges, more or less notched and sometimes hooked. The number and arrangement of skele-tal bones of the front and hind limbs are so variable that they were formerly used as a means of identification; but these are differences based on adaptation from an originally pen-tadactylous structure. Typical features are the columnar feet—elephantlike and covered with very thick, osteodermous scales in the land tortoises (Testudinidae)—and the feet suit-able for swimming, with free toes and developed webbing, in the pond turtles (for example, the Bataguridae and Emydidae). More distinctive still are the paddle-type forefeet of the Caret-tochelidae, Cheloniidae and Dermochelyidae.

The muscular system is very different from that of other land vertebrates; the presence of a rigid box around the body has modified the action of many of the original muscles, and these have become sufficiently strong to help move the neck, inside and outside the shell, and to move the limbs. In certain species, muscles have evolved with the capacity to open and close the plastron, which is completely or partially mobile compared with the carapace. Likewise, clear differences exist between the skeletal muscle, the cardiac muscle and the smooth muscles.

Respiratory system

These reptiles exhibit many variations in the anatomical and physiological specializations necessary for breathing, provid-ing an astonishing ability to fend off anoxia and the capacity to spend hours, weeks or even months submerged.

Knowledge about the physiology of respiration among che-lonians was for a long time merely approximate. Even though it was obvious from their anatomy that their type of breathing could not be the same as that of animals with an extendable thorax, experts sought to explain their methods of inhaling and exhaling—and hence of filling and emptying the lungs

The forelimb of a female *Trachemys scripta elegans,* one of the Emydidae.

Below, top to bottom: the head of two Testudinidae, Kinixys belliana *and* Testudo hermanni, *and of* Emys orbicularis *of the Emydidae.*

The head of an individual of the Trachemys *species: the rhythmic movement of the throat is only partly associated with respiration.*

(which are in the form of sacs with a variety of internal folds and chambers)—by resorting to analogies with other vertebrates. As in terrestrial amphibians, it was assumed that turtles breathed by virtue of the continuous movement of the hyoid bone, which operated like a pump to force air in and out of the lungs. The gullet movement of a frog is similar to that of a long-necked pond turtle; in both forms, the throat continuously swells and deflates.

It is now known, however, that the rhythmic contraction and relaxation of some of the muscles situated between the forelegs and beneath the intestines allow the air to be inhaled and exhaled. This is an action comparable to that of the diaphragm of mammals: one series of muscles behind the intestines pushes air from the nostrils into the pharynx; from there, it travels through the glottis to the larynx, the trachea and the two bronchi, which are linked to the respective lungs. Breathing out is effected by the reverse process: other muscles drive the

Thanks to the modification of their forelimbs, female marine turtles effect an astonishingly rapid return to the sea after depositing their eggs. Both photographs show individuals of Chelonia mydas.

intestines against the lungs, emptying them. This system, however, is hazardous. A simple drop in temperature may quickly lead to pneumonia by stopping the flow of mucus in the lungs.

Surviving underwater

A number of turtles of pond, sea and ocean are strong swimmers and have evolved alternative systems of breathing to enable them to survive underwater. Some species have a pharyngeal cavity covered with richly vascularized mucus, over which fresh water continuously flows. This permits an exchange of gases, which supplements the supply of oxygen to the blood (a system well developed in the softshell turtles and also the Cheloniidae and Dermochelyidae). Other species possess, on the inner sides of the cloaca, two introflexions with thin, well-capillarized walls (anal sacs), which work in the same way. This system of respiration, with rhythmic opening and closing movements of the cloaca, is highly developed in certain Chelidae. As a rule, though, resistance to immersion is not so remarkable; an active pond turtle cannot stay underwater for more than about half an hour, while a marine turtle interrupts its dive every 15 to 20 minutes to breathe at the surface. During winter dormancy, however, many turtles from temperate regions may bury themselves in the mud of a pond and manage to survive for two or three months without emerging. Marine turtles can remain submerged for entire days, resting on the bottom in a state of torpor. This astonishing feat is made possible not only by the supplementary breathing method mentioned above but also by the capacity to slow down internal metabolic rhythms and by the ability of the cardiac muscular tissue to operate for long periods, even with a shortage of oxygen.

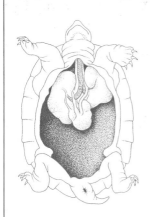

The respiratory and cardiac systems of a chelonian.

Circulatory system

Situated in a fairly forward position, between the two lungs and resting against the inner front part of the plastron, the heart of a turtle has only three chambers: two auricles and a single ventricle. Inside the ventricle is an incomplete septum that partially reduces the mixing of arterial and venous blood. Venous blood enters the heart through the right auricle. The auricle then contracts and pushes the blood into the right portion of the ventricle and from there into the pulmonary artery and through the left aortic arch. This action forces blood into the lungs, where carbon dioxide is removed and oxygen is added. The oxygenated blood then flows back into the left auricle through the pulmonary veins.

From the left auricle, the oxygenated blood flows into the left part of the ventricle and then through the right aortic arch and the dorsal aorta, reaching the entire body.

Period of activity

Like all reptiles, turtles and tortoises are ectothermic, or cold-blooded, and thus unable to maintain their body temperature independently of the outside temperature. For this reason, daily and seasonal temperatures regulate their vital activity; for exam-

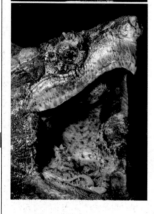

Below, the digestive system of a chelonian.

ple, some species enjoy basking in the sun during the early morning hours but will stay in the shade or in the water at the hottest times around midday. In temperate zones, activity is restricted to the warm months, while the cold season is spent buried deep in a place protected from temperature and water fluctuations. In dry regions or during periods of severe drought, there may be another phase of dormancy (estivation), when individuals bury themselves or retreat to the bottom of pools that are dry.

Digestive system

Turtles do not have teeth. They rely on their sharp jaws, which are covered by a notched or hooked horny beak that helps them to grasp plants or live prey and tear off small pieces with the aid of the forelimbs. The tongue, small, soft and fixed to the mouth cavity, is partially lubricated by the salivary glands. Food reaches the stomach through the glottis (which divides the respiratory tube from the alimentary canal) and the short esophageal tract (with very thin walls and an abundance of glands).

The intestine is divided into two parts by a pair of valves: the pyloric valve marks the entrance to the small intestine, while the ileocecal valve leads to the large intestine. Digestion is fairly slow, and the journey of the food from esophagus to stomach and thence to the intestine may take several hours. Many studies with pond turtles have shown that food remains in the esophagus for 3 to 4 hours, spends a further 8 to 10 hours in the stomach and takes another 20 hours or so to get through the intestine. The average digestion time for the Bataguridae and Emydidae is 72 hours, much less than that recorded for marine turtles (more than 170 hours for *Chelonia mydas*) or for the large land tortoises (almost 240 hours for the giant Aldabra tortoise *Aldabrachelys elephantina*). The feces are emitted through the cloaca, the opening that serves both the excretory and reproductive apparatus.

Food

The present-day species have omnivorous, carnivorous or herbivorous diets, the majority being omnivorous. Several carnivorous species are opportunists, feeding indifferently on live or dead prey, whatever is available. For example, after a downpour, *Terrapene* and *Rhinoclemmys* move to flooded ground to consume insect larvae and drowned earthworms.

Herbivorous species, too, may profit from the occasion by catching small snails and insect larvae or supplement the shortage of mineral salts in their diet by eating the feces of carnivores. In dry zones with scarce vegetation, land tortoises are adapted to feeding on extremely tough, thorny plants—*Geochelone sulcata* turns readily to brambles and acacias—and also consume the droppings of large herbivores. The leatherback can devour jellyfish with stinging tentacles. The alligator turtle

(*Macroclemys temminckii*) settles itself on the bottom, with jaws agape to reveal a fleshy, wormlike, mobile outgrowth on its tongue; the color and movement of this bait deceive small fishes to venture within range of its jaws. Many large Trionychidae are necrophagous, and because of this, a program in India aimed at repopulation favors certain species (*Aspideretes*, *Chitra* and *Pelochelys*) that can get rid of human corpses, which, by religious tradition, are thrown into the sacred waters of the river Ganges.

Excretory and reproductive system
The excretory apparatus of the Chelonia consists of two kidneys, each linked to a highly extensible vesicle situated near the cloaca. This holds the secretion of urine, which in the majority of species has some residue of nitrogenous urea. But life in extreme environments modifies this type of secretion: Among desert tortoises, for which water is too precious an asset to be eliminated, the secretion contains insoluble uric acid. Marine turtles, on the other hand, which are surrounded by seawater, expel mainly ammonia.

Present-day turtles and tortoises are of either sex and display a measure of sexual dimorphism. The females have two ovaries, which communicate with the cloaca via two oviducts. The presence of an apposite diverticulum in the cloaca enables her to store the spermatozoa transmitted during copulation for some time (in certain Testudinidae, even more than four years). Fertilization is internal, the males possessing a single large copulatory organ, highly dilatable, and situated, when relaxed, in the rear portion of the cloaca; sperm is ejaculated through the two vasa deferentia from the respective internal testicles.

Facing page, top to bottom: head of a Cuora species (Bataguridae), of Caretta caretta (Cheloniidae) and of Macroclemys temminckii (Chelydridae), with the characteristic wormlike appendage on the tongue.

Many tortoises and turtles exhibit distinct sexual dimorphism. As a rule, the major differences are in the length and thickness of the tail, greater in the male (seen on the right in the photograph below of a pair of Mauremys leprosa).

23

Reproduction
According to the environment and the climate, turtles and tortoises either concentrate their activity into short seasonal periods or distribute it evenly throughout the year. In this context, they may reproduce once or several times annually, with long or short spells of mating. Among the species of temperate climes (most of the Testudinidae and Emydidae), cou-

Top, two males of Gopherus agassizii *confront each other threateningly to determine territorial domination. Above, male land tortoises prepare for mating: top and center,* Testudo marginata; *bottom,* Testudo graeca.

plings occur in late spring; in those of tropical zones, they coincide with the pre-monsoon periods or take place year-round, reaching a peak in the warmest seasons.

Mating is often preceded by interesting prenuptial behavior, which tends to be precise and almost ritualized. Among the terrestrial tortoises, males spend a good deal of their active phase seeking out a possible partner. Having found a receptive female, one who is sexually mature and ready to reproduce, he will make his move in a spectacular and apparently violent manner. The female will be repeatedly nibbled on the neck and limbs or battered with his shell from every side in a whirling encounter that is only interrupted when he is certain of having persuaded her. At this point, he rears up on the female's body, gripping the rim of her carapace with his legs, and if she is compliant, copulation takes place. If the female has no intention of coupling, he will resume his assault. In the course of his onslaught, the male will emit loud snorts, hisses and gasps as air is rapidly forced out of his lungs.

Mating of aquatic turtles occurs differently and is not completely understood, given that it occurs in water—often at considerable depth—and at night. In many Emydidae of North America, the male swims repeatedly around the female, often coming to a halt in front of her and excitedly agitating his long-clawed forelimbs. This aquatic dance may continue for hours. Once seduced, the female permits him to mount her carapace, which he grips with his forelimbs, and lets him drag her along until the pair sink down deep in an embrace. In other aquatic species, the dance involves both sexes, each individual alternately coming to a halt while the other swims around the partner. In some cases, the male apparently profits from his potential mate's most stressful moments, as when a female marine turtle is forced to couple when she has only just completed the laborious and dangerous task of laying her eggs.

Egg laying and development

The Chelonia are oviparous, and their eggs are relatively big, with a calcareous, membranous shell, either soft and flexible or particularly hard and brittle. Number, shape and dimension vary according to the species and size of the female. For each clutch, the range is from a single egg for *Malacochersus tornieri*, 2 to 3 for *Testudo hermanni hermanni* and up to 80 or more for a marine turtle (Cheloniidae). In some cases, the female may produce a clutch several times during an active season, thus increasing the total number of eggs (200 or more for some individuals of *Chelonia mydas*). The shape of the egg may be elliptical or spherical, the coloration grayish or pure white, and the length up to about 7 cm (3 in).

The female has to face the difficulty, too, of locating a suitable place to lay her eggs and to oversee their subsequent development. At the same time, she must take into account the possibility of the young being forced to flee from predators and to reach a safe spot as quickly as they can. Experience that has accumulated over generations dictates that many species make their way year by year toward particular breeding areas; hence, any alteration in such a site may, in a very short time, result in the collapse of a turtle population.

After the eggs are laid, they are left to incubate naturally. Although there is an average limit to the process, the duration is strongly dependent on the weather and temperature in the ensuing months. The incubation period, in any event, differs even within populations of the same species, given that they may occupy geographical zones with variations in altitude, exposure and climate. As a rule, the eggs hatch within 70 to 90 days, but in many families, incubation may last much longer, even exceeding 200 days. Poor weather conditions may compel the newly hatched young to spend a period huddled in the nest or even inside the egg, thus prolonging the process, in some cases, for 6 to 7 months.

The average temperature at which the eggs are exposed dur-

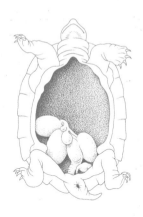

The reproductive system of a chelonian.

The eggs, the moment of hatching and the newborn of two of the best known European species of tortoise. Below, top and left, eggs and hatchlings of Emys orbicularis; *and below, center and bottom, of* Testudo hermanni.

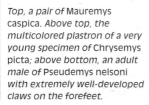

Top, a pair of Mauremys caspica. *Above top, the multicolored plastron of a very young specimen of* Chrysemys picta; *above bottom, an adult male of* Pseudemys nelsoni *with extremely well-developed claws on the forefeet.*

ing embryonic development may constitute a risk for the entire population. If it drops below a certain level (different for each species), the embryo will not grow. Moreover, when the average temperature hovers around 26° to 28°C (79°–83°F), a higher percentage of males will be born, whereas if it is above this average, the clutch will be prevalently female. This average incubation temperature to sex ratio does not always hold true, however, and numerous instances have been recorded where determination of sex is based on genetics.

Sexual dimorphism

While contrasts between the sexes are quite evident for certain species of Chelonia, in others, it is merely a matter of comparative size (females are generally bigger) that distinguishes them.

In the majority of the Testudinidae, the male's carapace is less convex, his head is proportionately larger, the supracaudal scutes face the abdomen, the plastron is concave, and the tail is longer, becoming broader and sturdier at the base.

These last two features likewise distinguish the males of many Emydidae, which are usually smaller than their partners. In some genera of this family (*Trachemys* and *Pseudemys*), the toes of the male's forelimbs are provided with long claws, up to 3 cm (1 in) long.

Examples of color dimorphism exist in every family, even though restricted to the breeding season, notably affecting the tones of the male's head and limbs. The males of certain species also develop unusual structures on the carapace, as well as longer gular scutes, more prominent keels, and ridges or hollows on the plastron (as in *Geochelone yniphora* and *Chersina angulata*).

Between the hatchlings and the young, there are few such clear distinctions: in most cases, the distance of the cloacal opening from the rear edge of the plastron (protecting the animal's abdomen) is greater in males.

Nervous and sensory systems

Turtles and tortoises possess three fundamental sensory organs: sight, taste and smell. The first is well developed; although laboratory tests have not determined to what extent turtles can distinguish colors, they have proved a preference for certain colors, such as orange and blue. It would appear that marine turtles find their way to the beaches they have picked out for laying their eggs by recognizing, often from the faint light of the stars, the shape of the coastline; and many pond turtles submerge themselves instantly at the least suspicious movement, just as they swim rapidly in the direction of any type of small prey that falls into the water.

Taste and smell are important in the search for food, to note the presence of a partner or an enemy, to recognize their own territory and to select the right place to build a nest. During the hunt for food, shelter or companion, a turtle continually gathers odorous particles in the air through the nostrils and the pharyngeal duct, which reach the olfactory epithelium situated on the choanae (internal nostrils). Here they are analyzed, furnishing the animal with the necessary information that will motivate its movements. If the smell signals the presence of food, the turtle will go and look for it; having found a potential meal, it will test its edibility (and this brings into play the taste cells scattered about the tongue).

In water, these senses are even more necessary, especially when it is cloudy or muddy and sight is useless (visibility is even further reduced by the lowering, when submerged, of the nictitating membrane that protects the eyes). For this rea-

son, aquatic species appear to grope their way forward, testing out at random whatever may seem to be edible or swallowing water to assess in the choanae the odorous traces carried in the liquid element. Hearing is practically worthless: as a rule, turtles "feel" the vibrations transmitted from the substratum and the water.

*Above, a red-eared pond slider (*Trachemys scripta elegans*). In fact, tortoises do not possess structures comparable to external ears. Below, a specimen of* Cistoclemmys galbinifrons.

PROBLEMS OF CONSERVATION

Problems of conservation

The present situation for many species of the Chelonia is critical. It may be that conservation initiatives, either currently in operation or planned, will prevent the disappearance of those most threatened. Although, in the recent past, few of these animals have become extinct because of direct human intervention, the dramatic alteration of many aquatic and terrestrial environments is bringing about an ever more rapid dwindling of populations. The factors that put turtles and tortoises at risk may be from natural or human causes, but whereas the former are well known and categorized, the consequences of the latter remain to be assessed. Thus far, the effects are discernible only in a few cases or in exceptional circumstances.

Previous spread, a pond turtle (Pseudemys sp.) *warms its body in apparent tranquillity on the back of a potential predator, the American alligator.*

The remains of young specimens of Testudo hermanni boettgeri *after a fatal raid in Dalmatia by herring gulls.*

THREATS FROM NATURAL CAUSES

In the course of their long evolution, which has seen them survive to this very day, chelonians have been confronted by innumerable cataclysms and upheavals affecting their environment. Climatic changes over the millennia have in turn worked to the advantage or disadvantage of one or another species. Yet a reasonable population level of these reptiles has been maintained in most continents that enjoy a temperate, tropical or subtropical climate, and there has been an acceptable presence of marine forms in the warm belts of the world's seas and oceans. So it is difficult to blame the disappearance of a population of turtles or tortoises on natural causes alone, even when this would seem to be the case. These animals exhibit a truly amazing measure of vitality. To ensure the future of the giant Aldabra turtle (*Aldabrachelys elephantina*), which at the end of the 19th century was practically extinct as a result of being hunted far and wide for its commercially profitable flesh, it was sufficient to put a halt to this cruel activity and put the Aldabra atoll under protection. Within 50 years, the local population of a few dozen specimens had, according to latest estimates, increased to around 130,000. As for the giant Galápagos tortoise, likewise on the brink of extinction, the saving factors have been efforts to decrease in predation of the young and the competition of herbivores (now numerous as a result of human introduction over the centuries of rats, pigs and goats).

Extremes of climate and temperature

Certain localized species in extremely hostile environments (such as *Geochelone sulcata* in the sub-Saharan region and *Gopherus agassizii* from northern Mexico) are placed at risk when long periods of

drought occur. Seasons of very heavy rain, with continual temperature fluctuations, may prevent successful breeding among many species in temperate zones, while high and low temperatures in the course of incubating the eggs may create, in the short term, a disproportion in the ratio of male to female hatchlings (notably in those species where determination of gender is dependent on average temperatures during the incubation period).

A good-size clutch of Chelonia mydas *eggs.*

Predation of eggs and young

The greatest natural danger to existing populations of chelonians is posed by predation of their eggs and young. The gamut of potential predators is huge, ranging from invertebrates (ants, for example, may invade the nests and gradually devour the embryos) to large and small mammals (carnivores, of course, but also rodents and insectivores relish this source of protein). In some cases, predation of the eggs may destroy 70 percent of the breeding potential of a species, to which must be added the killing of young at birth and during the first months of life (for a few species, it has been reckoned that a mere 1 to 2 percent of the young reach sexual maturity).

However, the excessive number of predators in some habitats is often associated with human interference, as in areas

administered by Europeans, where the concentration of animals and limited food resources result in the eggs and young of turtles being attacked by species that in other surroundings would not be ranked as specific predators (for instance, the badger and the jay). These same conditions serve to encourage predators thriving on human activity, such as rats and crows.

Above, all that remains of a nest of Emys orbicularis *after an attack by a fox; beside the shells is one successfully hatched individual of the same species, but this little turtle is still likely to encounter considerable danger.*

Predation of adults

Adults have fewer enemies than do the young: the presence of a strong bony shell is in itself a sufficient obstacle to predation; furthermore, turtles and tortoises profit from cryptic coloration, their capacity for passive resistance (if attacked, they retreat into their shell, fending off intruders for hours on end)

31

Some of the infections resulting from life in captivity (top to bottom): eye congestion due to polluted water, lack of vitamins and diet deficiencies; injuries and traumas caused by falls and bites by domesticated animals; and ulcers and infections due to poor care and untreated wounds.

and, among freshwater species, rapid flight toward water.

The hunters include a number of diurnal birds of prey, which have developed special tactics to capture and kill land tortoises (breaking open the shells by dropping them from a height onto the rocky ground), caimans and alligators, which feed contentedly on medium-size pond turtles.

Parasites and diseases

Various species of ticks (Ixodi) may attach themselves to the soft parts of tortoises and to the base of the limbs and tail. Barnacles and other marine invertebrates likewise cling to the carapace, plastron, limbs and head of sea turtles. Nematodes (roundworms), trematodes (flukes) and cestodes (tapeworms) feature among the many forms of internal parasites, but it is rare, unless the victim is debilitated for some other reason, for these to prove fatal. Working in a more underhand way are various bacteria, especially salmonella and mycobacterium, certain fungi, particularly *Mucor* and *Aspergillus*, and some viral infections of the *Herpesvirus* and *Papillomavirus* types. These cause diseases that undoubtedly affect the numbers of populations in the wild.

Other dangers

On the beaches where marine turtles nest, the eggs are subjected to the fluctuations of the tides and to the storms, which may literally drown the embryos; moreover, the growth of root systems of plants close to the nest may enmesh the eggs, hindering oxygenation or poisoning the embryos by emitting repellent substances. In some instances, overcrowding among female turtles laying their clutches may frustrate chances of successful breeding. The continuous and simultaneous arrival of thousands of individuals in a restricted area (as, for example, the *arribada* of *Lepidochelys olivacea* in Mexico) can cause disturbance to preceding nests, exposing the eggs to the elements.

HUMAN THREATS

Alterations to wet zones

Drainage and reclamation of wet zones are the principal causes of *Emys orbicularis* becoming rare in many countries of central and southern Europe, where, up to the end of the 19th century, these turtles were widely diffused in the huge ponds surrounding the mouths and estuaries of major rivers. The elimination of marshes, bogs and ponds similarly has led to a marked drop in numbers of certain Emydidae of North America, such as *Emydoidea blandingii* and *Clemmys marmorata*.

The creation of artificial irrigation networks, either above or below ground, the clearance of vegetation from watercourses

and along the banks, and excessive local use of water are likewise serious threats to the conservation of pond turtles. The clearance of the floating and shore vegetation of streams and rivers with rotary mowing machines causes the deaths of pond turtles basking in the sun; getting rid of vegetation also reduces the safety level of these animals, increasing the likelihood of attacks by predators and the drowning of hatchlings that are not yet capable of surviving strong currents and long periods underwater. Leveling and cementing of the banks reduce the quantity of food sources and of suitable sites for nesting and basking in the sun; the increased speed of the water flow prevents the buildup of sandy deposits and floating plant matter and makes the water too cold. The same problems confront the pond species as a result of constructing dams, locks and other devices designed to control the flow of water.

The dams under construction in Turkey across the Euphrates and Tigris Rivers are endangering the populations of *Trionyx triunguis* and *Rafetus euphraticus*, while other Trionychidae of Southeast Asia are swept away in the heavy flooding generated by dam building; many pond turtles end up dying wretchedly after falling into cemented-up canals. The use of reservoirs for irrigation purposes may cause sudden droughts that oblige the turtles to venture out on dangerous journeys toward other sites; and powerful irrigation pumps may suck up and kill very young turtles.

Extreme cases of human alteration to wet zones include straightening, cementing over and waterproofing of a riverbed; and the excavation of bed and banks for the transport of building materials.

Intensive farming
Vast territories have been denuded of animals in order to put land under extensive cultivation (notably for single crops such as cereals), and many species, particularly of the Testudinidae, have been forced to survive in narrow marginal areas of wasteland; this has happened to *Psammobates geometricus* and *Chersina angulata* in southern Africa and to *Testudo horsfieldi* along the Volga River in Russia.

Heavy losses are also due to modern methods of farming that involve the general use of machines for plowing, mowing, harrowing and the like.

Urban development
The massive development of towns and cities during the 20th century and the extensive breakup of natural habitats in order to build roads, railways and canals have had a grave effect on the chelonian populations of large urban areas. Because of the use of river sand for building, several Asiatic Bataguridae have vanished, having found it impossible to breed. Road traffic may eliminate individuals compelled to move from one part of a habitat to another, especially when the roads cut through wet zones or separate the pond environment from the sites used by these turtles for laying eggs. For years, the population of *Emys*

Vast areas of plain in the Western world have been irreversibly destroyed by intensive farming and cementing.

Thousands of acres of forest are destroyed every year throughout the world as land is converted for short-term agricultural use. Land tortoises are among the millions of small victims. Above, a specimen of Testudo hermanni *that miraculously survived a coastal fire in Italy.*

*Chemical pollution endangers the life of the few turtles that manage to survive. Right, a young green turtle (*Chelonia mydas*) is rescued in a drag net.*

orbicularis of the wet coastal regions of the area surrounding Ravenna, Italy, was decimated as the animals risked crossing the Romea state highway (until suitable barriers were built in 1995). Hundreds of *Gopherus polyphemus* and *Malaclemys terrapin* are killed every year on the highways of Florida and the eastern United States, protected only by short tracts of barrier. The presence of coastal roads also proves critical for the breeding chances of marine turtles: car headlights, in fact, may ensnare the small turtles as they leave the nest, leading them onto the road rather than toward safety in the sea. The destructive impact of an autoroute on the population of *Testudo hermanni* in the Mauri Massif of France has likewise been lessened by the construction of barriers and the building of viaducts.

Deforestation and fires

Some turtle species are gravely threatened when tropical forests are cut down and destroyed to create makeshift patches of cultivation or to obtain valuable timber: in Africa (*Kinixys homeana* in the Ivory Coast), in eastern Asia (*Cistoclemmys galbinifrons* in Vietnam) and in South America (*Geochelone carbonaria* and *G. denticulata* in Brazil). Equally devastating for the land tortoises of other countries is the removal of vegetational cover, both shrubs and trees. The range of *Testudo hermanni hermanni* has shrunk along the coasts of Spain, France and Italy, as belts of garrigue and Mediterranean maquis have been eliminated. Fires in woods and forests likewise pose a terrible threat to animals unable to flee. The land tortoises of the Mediterranean are among the principal victims of the destructive summer fires that rage across the maquis and the coastal pine forests.

Pollution

Little is known about the harm done to terrestrial and aquatic species as a result of spilling chemical substances into the water, ground or atmosphere. However, scientists have confirmed the lethal effects from the use of herbicides in agriculture, such as 2.4.D and 2.5.T and atrazine (on *Testudo hermanni boettgeri* in Greece). The European pond turtles (*Emys orbicularis*, *Mauremys leprosa* and *M. rivulata*), which live in water with overabundant plant growth as a result of pollution and often with additional pollution from chemical wastes, exhibit a variety of pathological symptoms or the growth of crustlike parasitic algae on their shells.

Some species of *Graptemys* in the

United States are seriously endangered by the progressive modification of the waters in which they live. And as a result of catastrophic spills into the sea of naphtha and oil from fuel tankers, many marine turtles (*Chelonia mydas*, in particular) have been found dying and dead.

Trade in food and traditional medicine

For centuries, the Chelonia have been a source of protein in the diets of humans living in hostile or isolated environments, and even today in various parts of the world, the hunting and capture of turtles and tortoises for direct consumption is a normal activity. But it is only in places where collecting these animals has assumed commercial proportions that the species involved have seen their numbers decimated or entire populations wiped out. This has happened to the large terrestrial tortoises living on islands, such as *Aldabrachelys elephantina* and *Geochelone nigra*, which were brought to the verge of extinction between 1700 and 1900 as the crews of ships, plying the oceans on voyages of trade or exploration, indulged in the relentless pursuit and capture of the animals. The same fate was suffered by marine turtles, especially the green turtle (*Chelonia mydas*), which were caught and removed in vast numbers as they assembled at their breeding sites on the beaches; the delicacies sought by the thieves were not only the meat and calipee (the fatty substance on the limbs above the pastron) but also the horny plates or entire shell. Furthermore, a vast number die each year as a result of commercial fishing (trawling and seining). To reduce the potential carnage in American waters, this type of fishing is permitted only when accompanied by an automatic system of freeing the trapped turtles. The collection of eggs after nest building has wiped out several populations of *Chelonia mydas* and Dermochelyidae of the Malaysian peninsula, Indonesia and the Philippines.

Persecution is also the lot of the large pond turtles of eastern Australia (*Chitra, Aspideretes, Pelochelys, Callagur, Batagur, Orlitia*) and of South America (*Podocnemis* spp., *Chelus fimbriatus*). These creatures are caught directly with nets, lines, large hooks or harpoons and brought to local markets or exported. Southern China is today the center of commerce for meat and by-products (above all for traditional medicines), and it is here that millions of specimens of turtles and

Left and above, three factors that constitute the gravest threats to tortoises and turtles: the theft of eggs and adult animals for food (eggs of Chelonia mydas *in a Malaysian market); the use of fishing methods that prevent the migrations and entrap marine turtles; and the capture of rare specimens for collections.*

One of the most recently described turtle species, Cuora zhoui, *below, from southern China, is already in extreme danger.*

35

Tragic aspects of the international traffic in turtles: top, holding cages for air transport; above, three examples of Bataguridae found dead from the torment of captivity in the course of one such flight.

Stuffed bodies of marine turtles confiscated at the frontier from travelers unaware of the CITES prohibitions.

tortoises captured in Laos, Vietnam, Malaysia, Cambodia, Bangladesh and Indonesia arrive to be sold at high prices.

Exhibits and pets

Chelonians are nowadays a prime object of commerce for sale as pets and terrarium specimens. From 1950 to 1960, trading centers in eastern Asia coordinated this traffic, bringing together the captors and provisional breeders of these animals with the wholesalers and exporters.

Buyers in the West would signal their preference for those species, whether common or rare, which displayed unusually attractive colors and patterns (*Cuora zhoui, C. mccordi, C. pani*). In certain cases (*Cuora aurocapitata*), to maintain high sale prices, wild specimens were caught indiscriminately, kept in captivity and dispatched a few at a time to international buyers.

To aid and abet this traffic, centers of intensive breeding were set up—virtual turtle farms—specializing in producing the species in greatest demand. The best known of these establishments are in the United States, which for more than 30 years has led the field in this form of commerce, flooding the international market with the hatchlings of one showy member of the Emydidae, *Trachemys scripta elegans*. Some six million specimens a year find their way to markets in Asia and Europe, a very high percentage of which are subsequently set loose without thought or discrimination in wet zones, both natural and artificial, resulting in a form of wildlife contamination that is unique worldwide. Yet it is often insufficient to meet demand, and there is still widespread recourse to direct-capture turtles or harvest eggs in the wild; this is why many species that are commonly on sale as pets in Western countries are becoming rare or almost extinct in their lands of origin (this is the case, too, with some local races of *Trachemys scripta elegans*).

Innumerable individuals do not survive the first few days after being captured (kept in overcrowded, makeshift accommodation before being dispatched to the wholesalers for shipment), and many others die in the course of the journey abroad (often in terrible conditions), in the tanks of the importers or in the hands of inexpert breeders. Such traffic has to some extent been checked by the establishment of international conven-

tions on trade in wild animals, but the number of species taken into consideration is too few in the light of those still under threat.

PROTECTIVE LEGISLATION

Since 1971, the signing of international conventions by the governments of many nations has somewhat eased the situation of the Chelonia. On February 2, 1971, the Ramsar Convention for the safeguarding and wise use of wetlands was adopted. Although it was aimed at the conservation of the habitats of aquatic birds, it was also designed to protect all the animals in the world's major wetlands. On April 30, 1973, CITES, the Convention on International Trade in Endangered Species of Wild Fauna and Flora, was signed in Washington. This treaty provides for scientific control and scrupulous administration in every individual case involving the import or export of protected plants and animals, carrying heavy fines and penalties for any eventual breaches and irregularities.

The species under consideration, which nevertheless constitute only a minimal part of those that make up international traffic, are catalogued in appendices according to their level of protection and therefore of commercial restriction. Appendix I lists the species most at risk, for which commerce is as a rule completely prohibited, while Appendices II and III list respectively endangered species for which international commerce is restricted or controlled, or those for which one nation alone has requested trade restrictions (see Table 1 for the chelonian species taken into account).

The lists are periodically brought up to date, and if need be, the levels of protection are modified and set out in various appendices. But the lack of data concerning the situation in the wild of a large number of species prevents their timely consideration and inclusion; consequently, it is all too likely that some species will be wiped out by excessive

Another consequence of the traffic in wild animals is the large-scale abandonment of turtles in non-native habitats by bored pet owners. The case of specimens of Trachemys scripta elegans *that have grown too big is all too familiar (below, only five years separate these two individuals). Even so, pet shops are always on the lookout for new species to attract potential customers, who may eventually abandon them (bottom, newborn specimens of* Chrysemys picta, Pseudemys concinna, Pseudemys floridana *and* Graptemys khonii).

Table 1

Table 1. The species of European Chelonia listed in the CITES Appendices, with the redefinition by the EC (based upon the European Community Regulation no. 338/97 of 9.12.1996).

Appendix I

Bataguridae	*Batagur baska*
	Geoclemys hamiltonii
	Melanochelys tricarinata
	Kachuga tecta
	Morenia ocellata
Emydidae	*Terrapene cohauila*
Testudinidae	*Geochelone nigra* (= *elephantopus*)
	Geochelone radiata
	Geochelone yniphora
	Psammobates geometricus

- *Testudo hermanni* All. A/CE
- *Testudo graeca* All. A/CE
- *Testudo marginata* All. A/CE

Cheloniidae	*Eretmochelys imbricata*
	Lepidochelys kempii
Trionychidae	*Lissemys punctata punctata*
	Apalone spiniferus ater
	Aspideretes nigricans
	Aspideretes gangeticus
	Aspideretes hurum
Chelidae	*Pseudemydura umbrina*

A snapping turtle (Chelydra serpentina): this species appears with Mauremys caspica and Macroclemys temminckii in the lists of species considered to be endangered and thus not available for breeding and commerce.

depredation and commerce even before they are catalogued (as is happening in southern China with certain species of the genus *Cuora*, such as *C. zhoui* and *C. aurocapitata*). For the states of the European Community (EEC), a new ruling was introduced in June 1997, with a redefining of the lists of species under consideration into four categories (A, B, C and D).

On September 19, 1979, the convention for the conservation of European fauna and flora and their habitats was signed at Berne. Each nation is obliged by this law to protect those fauna and flora species judged to require priority action; every species that is listed is safeguarded against instances of killing, capture, detention and commerce, and their habitats guaranteed the most suitable measures of conservation. With DPR. no. 357 of 8.9.1977 (Ordinary Supplement of Official Gazette 248 of 23.10.1997, N. 218/l), "Regulation for realization of EU

Table 2 Species of Chelonia given priority by the EU

Category II

Testudinata	Emydidae	*Emys orbicularis*
	Bataguridae	*Mauremys leprosa*
		Mauremys rivulata
		Mauremys caspica
	Testudinidae	*Testudo hermanni*
		Testudo graeca
	Cheloniidae	*Caretta caretta*
		Chelonia mydas
		Eretmochelys imbricata
		Lepidochelys kempii
	Dermochelyidae	*Dermochelys coriacea*

Appendix II		Appendix III	
Emydidae	*Clemmys muhlenbergii*	Trionychidae	*Trionyx triunguis*
	Terrapene spp.		*Pelomedusa subrufa*
• *Trachemys scripta elegans* All. B/CE			*Pelusios adansonii*
Testudinidae	*Chersina angulata*		*Pelusios castaneus*
	Aldabrachelys elephantina		*Pelusios gabonensis*
	Geochelone spp.		*Pelusios niger*
	Indotestudo spp.		
	Gopherus spp.		
	Homopus spp.		
	Kinixys spp.		
	Manouria spp.		
	Malacochersus spp.		
	Pyxis spp.		
	Testudo spp.		
Dermatemydidae	*Dermatemys mawii*		
Pelomedusidae	*Podocnemis* spp.		
	Erymnochelys madagascariensis		
	Peltocephalus dumerilianus		

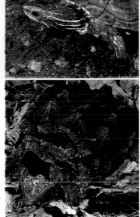

directive 92/43 regarding conservation of natural and semi-natural habitats, as well as wild fauna and flora," Italy finally ratified the EU directive 1992/43 entitled "Habitat," designed to preserve habitats and animal and plant species considered of public importance (see documents A and B of DPR no. 357, corresponding to documents I and H of directive 92/43).

The supervision of everything related to this order was entrusted to the State Forestry Department. However, there are to date no specific prohibitions or any envisaged sanctions against noncompliance (Table 2 shows the list of Chelonia given priority by the EU).

Various nations today have laws that guarantee the security of chelonians or deal specifically with their protection; it is not possible to mention them all here, but reference is made to some of them in the individual entries.

The Decree of 19.4.1996, with its list of animal species that may represent a danger to public health and safety and the detention of which is prohibited (GU no. 232 of 3.10.1996), effectively puts a halt to importation and the free sale of species considered a threat to humans. Among the chelonians listed are the snapping turtles of the family Chelydridae (*Chelydra serpentina* and *Macroclemys temminckii*) and, for health reasons, one of the Bataguridae *Mauremys caspica*).

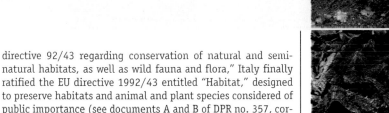

Top, Mauremys caspica; *above*, Macroclemys temminckii.

SEAS AND OCEANS

Originally inhabitants of ponds, swamps and lagoons, the Chelonia gradually conquered large parts of the surrounding areas of dry land. Some groups, however, took an evolutionary step backwards and perfected their adaptations to the watery element to become masters of the most immense areas of the Earth's surface, the seas and oceans.

Two families of marine turtles exist today, diffused principally in tropical and subtropical waters: the Cheloniidae, with six species, and the Dermochelyidae, with just one species.

These are reptiles of moderate or large size, worthy descendants of the gigantic chelonians that swam the Cretaceous seas, such as *Archelon ischyros*, with a shell of more than 3 m (10 ft) in length. Other characteristics are decidedly primitive, notably the inability to retract the head and limbs inside the shell, the closed back of the skull and the complete series of inframarginal plates between scute and plastron. The shape of the head, however, is specialized, perfectly hydrodynamic, as are the forelimbs, transformed into swim paddles for swift movement and maneuvering.

Despite their uniform appearance and living environment, the existing marine turtles favor their own particular diet (which has led to a significant diversity in the form and consistency of their jaw surface); they also select a variety of beaches for laying their eggs (or when, by force of circumstance, the choice is for a single breeding site, the eggs are laid at different periods); and they frequent water at varying distances from the coast. As a rule, though, they tend to swim close to the shore, making for the open sea only when they move from a feeding zone to a breeding area, which may sometimes be more than 1,500 to 2,000 km (900–1,200 miles) apart; only the leatherback (*Dermochelys coriacea*) leads a life that is almost exclusively pelagic.

After surviving millions of years apparently without problems, these reptiles have been brought to the brink of extinc-

The great marine turtles are the best-equipped modern-day reptiles to adapt to the marine environment, where they lead a solitary existence, traveling immense distances. They migrate from the feeding grounds to the breeding sites, which may be hundreds of miles apart. Previous spread, a female green turtle (Chelonia mydas) returning to the water after depositing her eggs.

tion in only a couple of centuries. The reasons are that they have been hunted relentlessly for food and killed indiscriminately by ships' propellers and in fishing nets; excessive harvesting of eggs and the elimination of places to land and nest on beaches, which have been converted into tourist areas, have also led to this critical situation. This is why dozens of programs have been initiated to save many of the surviving populations, supported by apposite international legislation.

Marine turtles assemble only once a year in places suitable for reproduction. The males patrol the coasts where the females gather to lay their eggs, and await them in preparation to couple again (a pair of green turtles appear below).

CHELONIIDAE

This family contains those marine turtles with a shell covered by large horny plates. The seven known species belong to five genera: *Chelonia, Natator, Eretmochelys, Caretta* and *Lepidochelys*. These are reptiles highly adapted to aquatic life, and only the females come onto land for brief periods during egg laying, while mating takes place in the sea, even if only a short distance from shore.

The female Cheloniidae venture onto land mainly at night and, having reached their chosen site, excavate a large hollow with their forefeet; then, with their hind feet, and much more delicately, they scoop out the center to form a small hole about 30 cm (12 in) deep, which is the nest chamber. They moisten this with a watery excretion from the cloaca prior to depositing their almost spherical eggs—anywhere from 12 to more than 200, depending

43

on the species, the age and the size of the female. During the active season, there may be several clutches (up to five) some 10 to 15 days apart. When they have finished laying, the females carefully fill the nest with sand, leveling and pressing down the entire zone to wipe out all traces before returning to the sea; the whole process takes a couple of hours or so. The eggs incubate naturally within about two months, and the young hatch at night, all together, immediately plunging into the water. The diet varies according to species: *Chelonia mydas*, *C. agassizii* and *Natator depressa* are mainly herbivores, feeding on aquatic plants and marine algae (*Zostera*, *Sargassum*, *Sagittaria*, *Vallisneria*, *Ulva*, *Thalassia* and *Posidonia*); other species, such as *Eretmochelys imbricata*, are omnivorous, with a preference for fish, mollusks and crustaceans; *Lepidochelys* supplements aquatic vegetation and marine algae with small crustaceans, mollusks and fish; and *Caretta* feeds mainly on sponges, tunicates, mollusks and crustaceans.

*After her dangerous and exhausting egg-laying mission, a large female green turtle, top, resumes life in the sea, leaving 200 or more eggs well hidden in a hole excavated on the beach. A loggerhead (*Caretta caretta*), right, has almost finished its meal of a large crayfish.*

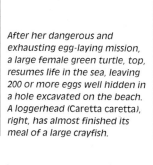

Identifying the genera of present-day marine turtles

1. Large size, over 200 cm (80 in); body covered with small, juxtaposed bony plates set into the thick epidermis → Dermochelys.

1a. Medium size, exceptionally over 150 cm (60 in); shell covered with large horny scutes → 2.

2. Four pairs of pleural scutes on each side of the carapace; cervical scute does not touch first pleural scute → 3.

2a. Five or more pairs of pleural scutes on each side of the carapace; cervical scute touches first pleural scute → 5.

3. Three postocular scales → Natator.

3a. Four postocular scales → 4.

4. One pair of prefrontal scales → Chelonia.

4a. Two pairs of prefrontal scales; scutes of carapace markedly imbricate → Eretmochelys.

5. Bridge with three large inframarginals; scutes of carapace not imbricate except for very young specimens; color brownish or reddish brown → Caretta.

5a. Bridge with four large inframarginals, some or all with pores; color gray to olive-green → Lepidochelys.

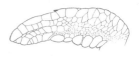

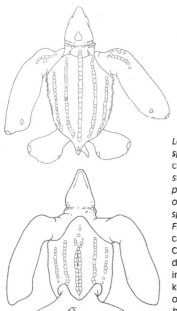

Left, back and belly of a young specimen of Dermochelys coriacea. Right, form and structure (showing shape and position of scales and claws) of the forelimbs in various species of Cheloniidae. From top to bottom: Caretta caretta, Chelonia mydas, Chelonia agassizii, Natator depressa, Eretmochelys imbricata, Lepidochelys kempii and Lepidochelys olivacea (based on drawings by CITES, 1995).

Loggerhead turtle
Caretta caretta (Linnaeus, 1758)

Family
Cheloniidae.
Distribution and habitat
Mediterranean, Caribbean, Atlantic, Pacific and Indian Oceans, in the temperate subtropical and tropical belts. It may venture a considerable distance from the coast at moderate depth—240 km (150 miles) and over 100 m (330 ft)—but as a rule stays close to rocky shores, lagoons, large bays and river mouths.

The loggerhead breeds principally on beaches of temperate zones, often coming ashore after long migrations that carry them far from their feeding grounds.

Characteristics
The carapace may measure over 200 cm (80 in) long, the maximum observed being 213 cm (84 in), with a weight of 100 to 150 kg (220–330 lb), up to 450 kg (1,000 lb) in large individuals. The elongate carapace is reddish brown or olive-green, the scutes bordered yellow. Bridge and plastron are creamy yellow.

Mating occurs in the proximity of the beaches chosen for deposition of eggs; this may happen either by day or by night and is repeated up to six times during an active season, about once a fortnight. The eggs are laid in a chamber dug out to a depth of around 20 cm (8 in). They are spherical, 35

to 49 mm (1½–2 in), with up to 200 in a clutch. Incubation lasts 50 to 70 days. The young, which at birth do not measure more than 55 mm (2 in), break free and then make for the sea during the night.

Food is omnivorous, basically marine invertebrates, fish and algae (*Zostera*, *Thalassia* and *Sargassum*). Some populations may spend cold periods hibernating on the seabed.

Situation *Caretta caretta* is one of the most endangered marine turtle species; many of its breeding sites have disappeared as a result of habitat modification and the massive influx of tourists along the coasts.

It is listed in Appendix I of CITES, in Appendix II of the Berne Convention, and is described as "Threatened" under the U.S. Endangered Species Act. Many projects for conservation and census taking have been initiated in recent years in the Mediterranean and elsewhere.

There are two known subspecies of Caretta caretta. Caretta c. caretta, *above, comes from the Atlantic and the Mediterranean.* Caretta c. gigas, *below, from the Pacific and Indian Oceans.*

Green turtle
Chelonia mydas (Linnaeus, 1758)

2

Family
Cheloniidae.
Distribution and habitat
Tropical waters of Atlantic, Pacific and Indian Oceans, but also

found off colder shorelines such as Great Britain and, very rarely, in the Mediterranean, especially off the

north and west coasts of Africa. It also lives in the open seas and off shores with plenty of submerged vegetation.

Characteristics The carapace, up to 150 cm (60 in), has olive-green or brown scutes, often with a radial pattern or a scattering of dark marblings. The plastron, however, is very pale, almost white. The weight in large specimens may exceed 300 kg (660 lb). The head has just two prefrontal scales, and there is a horny, notched spur on the jaws. Breeding takes place on many beaches in Central America, islands of the western Pacific,

India and Southeast Asia. The turtle seeks its food along the shores, showing a preference for aquatic phanerogams such as *Zostera* and *Thalassia* (which grow on sandy seabeds) but often supplementing this diet with marine algae and mollusks. Although it lives mainly close to the shore, it will readily embark on transoceanic migrations of more than 2,000 km (1,200 miles) to reach its breeding sites. The female lays 85 to 200 eggs per clutch, 3 to 5 times a season at intervals of 2 to 3 weeks. The turtles are easily observable when they feed in the shallows or let themselves be rocked

lazily by the waves as they float at the surface.

Situation It is listed in CITES Appendix I, in Appendix II of the Berne Convention and as "Threatened" under the U.S. Endangered Species Act.

In terms of number of eggs per single clutch, the green turtle is the most prolific of present-day turtles; large females may lay more than 200 eggs annually on the beaches of Costa Rica. The figures, however, are misleading, since the majority of hatchlings die during the first few months of life.

Agassiz's green turtle
Chelonia agassizii (Bocourt, 1868)

3

50

Family Cheloniidae.
Distribution and habitat Often associated with *Chelonia mydas*, of which it was considered a subspecies until a few years ago. Lives in the eastern Pacific from California to Chile, west to the Galápagos and Papua New Guinea. Large concentrations gather along the Australian Great Barrier Reef.

Characteristics It is on average much smaller and lighter in weight than its relative, and thus fewer eggs are laid in each clutch (around 80 at the Galápagos breeding sites). The deposition period varies according to place (in Australia from October to February, in Sri Lanka from July to November). The females come ashore at night and

often take advantage of the change of tide. This species, too, has an omnivorous diet, but the very young are prevalently carnivores, feeding on zooplankton.
Situation Hunting of adults and harvesting of eggs have seriously threatened the populations of Southeast Asia. The highly interesting populations of the Galápagos (in the photograph, several females are seen leaving the beach where they have just reproduced) are today at grave risk because of the predation of eggs and young by animals previously introduced by man. It is listed in CITES Appendix I.

Flat-back turtle
Natator depressa
(Garman, 1880)

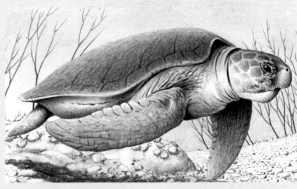

Family Cheloniidae.
Distribution and habitat Open seas and along the coral reefs of Australia and New Guinea.
Characteristics The carapace is up to 100 cm (40 in) long; the scutes of the plastron and bridge creamy white and unspotted. Unlike the species of the genus *Chelonia*, the females seem to prefer the daylight hours to lay their eggs, which are always fewer in number (an average of 50 per clutch), though somewhat bigger. It breeds along the beaches of northern and eastern Australia. Incubation lasts about 6 weeks, and the hatchlings emerge at night. More carnivorous than *Chelonia mydas*, it feeds on various types of marine invertebrates.
Situation It is protected under CITES Appendix I. The turtle is less likely than other species to be taken directly for food and commerce.

Kemp's ridley turtle
Lepidochelys kempii
(Garman, 1880)

Family Cheloniidae.
Distribution and habitat Western Atlantic from Nova Scotia to Gulf of Mexico. It may also range in the eastern Atlantic as far as Europe and is occasionally found in the Mediterranean. It frequents coastal waters, especially lagoons and tranquil bays.
Characteristics It is a small marine turtle that barely grows to 70 cm (28 in). It typically breeds annually, from April to August, several hundred females to a group. Each clutch comprises 80 to 140 eggs. Prevalently carnivorous, it feeds on clams, snails, jellyfish, crabs and fish.
Situation The most threatened marine turtle today, it has been decimated by direct capture and the effects of trawling and other fishing methods. The known breeding sites of the species are also under threat, limited as they are to the Mexican coasts around Rancho Nuevo in Tamaulipas state. It is protected under CITES Appendix I.

Olive ridley turtle
Lepidochelys olivacea (Eschscholtz, 1829)

4

Family Cheloniidae.
Distribution and habitat Tropical waters of the Pacific and Indian Oceans and also of the Atlantic Ocean (western coast of Africa and northern coast of South America). It primarily lives close to shore, especially in shallow, sheltered water, but is occasionally found in the open sea; it also frequents coastal lagoons.
Characteristics One of the smallest marine turtles, its maximum known size is around 71 cm (28 in). The various populations, north and south of the equator, breed in different months (July to November in Mexico). They assemble in large numbers on the beaches of Orissa (India), with up to 100,000 nests counted every year. Two clutches, each of about 100 eggs, are deposited during the breeding season, females taking an hour or so to complete the task. Incubation lasts approximately 50 to 60 days.

The diet is almost wholly carnivorous, based primarily on fish, mollusks and crustaceans.

Situation After near extermination in the recent past, today the species has recovered its numbers, and the majority of its breeding sites are protected. Only a few years ago, it was the most endangered species along the Pacific coasts of Mexico and Central America (in the 1970s, about a million are said to have been killed in Mexico alone).

The government of Cuba was the first, in 1968, to prohibit the trade in captured and slaughtered turtles, and the transformed situation of the species has also been confirmed by chelonian world specialist P. C. H. Pritchard. Nowadays, the concentrations of breeding females constitute a guaranteed and profitable influx of tourists for local inhabitants. The species is listed in CITES Appendix I.

Hawksbill turtle
Eretmochelys imbricata (Linnaeus, 1766)

5

53

Family Cheloniidae.
Distribution and habitat
Lives in all tropical seas
and oceans and often in
temperate waters (it may
reach the coasts of Scot-
land and Morocco but is
rare in the Mediterranean).

The two known sub-
species are *E. i. imbricata*
and *E. i. bissa*. They prefer
rocky coastlines, mangrove
ponds and the teeming
waters around coral reefs.
Characteristics It grows to
less than 100 cm (40 in) in
length, the maximum
recorded being 91 cm (3 ft).
In young specimens, the
overlapping scales of the
carapace are very marked.

Mating occurs just off
the beaches used by the
females for nesting, which
takes place at night. Digging of the nest, deposi-
tion of the eggs (up to 160)
and return to the sea are
completed within an hour
or so. The female's reproductive cycle is triennial.

The young hatch within

about 60 days. The diet is
omnivorous, with a high
proportion of marine invertebrates.
Situation Killing—in order
to remove the valuable
horny plates of the cara-
pace—and filching of eggs
on breeding sites represent
grave threats to this handsome species. To protect at
least a part of its population, it has been listed in
CITES Appendix I and is
one of the priority species
for conservation in Europe
(Berne and Habitat Con-
ventions) and America
(U.S. Endangered Species
Act). It is listed as "Endangered" in the IUCN Red
Data Book.

Having only emerged from the egg a few hours previously, this baby leatherback struggles frantically to reach the sea and thus avoid becoming a meal for a crab, vulture, frigate bird, gull or wild pig. Measuring scarcely 60 mm (2½ in), it is, for the time being, only a miniature version of one of the biggest living reptiles.

DERMOCHELYIDAE

The sole representative of this family, *Dermochelys coriacea* is virtually the only living reptile with a range that is almost exclusively pelagic, inhabiting all tropical and temperate seas. The carapace consists of innumerable juxtaposed small bony plates set into the thick, leathery skin and almost completely lacks an exoskeleton. The head is huge, with jaws covered by horny hooked spurs.

As to their origin, one school of thought is that this family constitutes an ancestral line which separated from the principal stock of the Chelonia as long ago as the Triassic; the second theory is that it broke away from the main line of the Thecophora through the marine turtles of the genus *Archelon* (belonging to the extinct family of Protostegidae), which lived in the Upper Cretaceous, and from a similar giant reptile of the same period.

Veritable giants of the seas and oceans, leatherbacks come ashore only to lay their eggs. Leaving the water is the most arduous and dangerous event of their life; a number of individuals drown every year near the breeding sites either from exhaustion or from being overcome in the sun by heatstroke.

Leatherback turtle
Dermochelys coriacea (Vandelli, 1761)

6

Family Dermochelyidae.
Distribution and habitat
Present in nearly all the world's seas and oceans, with a preference for tropical and subtropical waters, but also ranges into the cold waters of Alaska, Labrador and Iceland. The two known subspecies are *D. c. coriacea* and *D. c. schlegelii*. It breeds mainly on the beaches of Central America and of northwest Africa. The largest breeding colonies are to be found on the beach of Yalimapo, in French Guiana (Kawana Turtle Project). Basically, it is a pelagic animal that seldom visits the shore.

Characteristics The leather back is the largest living turtle, and it is not uncommon to come across individuals measuring over 2 m (6½ ft) in length, the maximum being 244 cm (8 ft), and weighing more than 500 kg (1,100 lb), with a maximum of 659 kg (1,500 lb). The females (between May and June in Surinam) come ashore 3 to 7 times a year, at intervals of 6 to 10 days, to lay their eggs, 50 to 170 at a time. Incubation takes 60 to 70 days. The diet is omnivorous, with a clear preference for coelenterates and cephalopods.
Situation Its survival is threatened by a marked

reduction of suitable breeding zones and direct deaths as a result of colliding with the propellers of powerboats.

Several nations have introduced measures for safeguarding breeding sites (French Guiana, Costa Rica, Mexico, South Africa, Sri Lanka, Australia, Trinidad, Tobago and Surinam). It appears in CITES Appendix I and in Appendix II of the Berne Convention and is considered "Endangered" under the U.S. Endangered Species Act.

PALEARCTIC SUBREGION

PALEARCTIC SUBREGION

Europe, North Africa, Asia to transition zone with China, and Japan

There are seven native species of European turtles and tortoises, belonging to three families: Emydidae, with *Emys orbicularis*, Bataguridae, with *Mauremys caspica* and *M. leprosa*, and Testudinidae, with *Testudo hermanni*, *T. graeca*, *T. marginata* and *T. (=Agrionemys) horsfieldi*.

The European pond turtles are the most widely distributed but also the most seriously threatened and thus the object of many conservation programs.

The land tortoises live along the Mediterranean basin from southern Spain to France, Italy and Sicily; the Ionian and Adriatic shorelines (smaller populations to the north); and the coasts of Dalmatia and Herzegovina, Albania, Macedonia, Greece and Turkey. Their original range has been greatly reduced as a result of human activity, even though this has benefited certain species, which have been released from cap-

Centuries of human pressure have almost totally transformed the European natural landscape, where endemic land tortoises survive in marginal enclaves between cultivated zones and built-up areas. Broadly speaking, many of the species concerned, such as Testudo hermanni, *shown on the previous spread, have continually been hounded for commercial traffic, and it is now difficult even to trace the extent of their original range.*

tivity and commerce into the wild. The northernmost limit of original distribution is that of *Testudo horsfieldi*, which is found in Kazakhstan at 52°N; and *Emys orbicularis* has been reintroduced to Lithuania even in places up to 57°N.

The pond slider (*Trachemys scripta elegans*) is now regarded as a European species, though originally from North America, for it has been naturalized in some areas of southern France and central Italy. Widely sold as a pet, hundreds have been abandoned and found their way back to natural wet zones.

Among the chelonian species of the western Palearctic, albeit marginally, are two Trionychidae: *Rafetus euphraticus* (in Turkey, Iraq and Iran) and *Trionyx triunguis* (in Africa and Turkey); *Testudo graeca* and *Mauremys leprosa* are found on all sides of the Mediterranean basin.

The smallest species of the genus *Testudo*, *T. kleinmanni*, also lives along the Mediterranean shores of North Africa.

The eastern Palearctic subregion, however, despite its vast extent, contains surprisingly few chelonians, and in over the greater part of its territory, they are wholly absent.

Testudo horsfieldi also occurs from the Caspian Sea to Baluchistan, while several forms of *T. graeca* are present along the Turkish border with Afghanistan.

Characteristic species of the Bataguridae, such as *Chinemys reevesii* and *Mauremys japonica*, are found only in southern China, Japan and on some of its smaller islands.

The wet zones of Europe have been subjected to such drastic modification over the years that it is hard to imagine what the original habitats of these reptiles looked like. The transformation continues apace and forces the creatures into ever more constricted areas. For this reason, the few species of European freshwater turtles are gravely threatened, the focus of various laborious and costly programs of conservation.

European pond turtle

Emys orbicularis (Linnaeus, 1758)

7

Family Emydidae.
Distribution and habitat The original immense area of distribution  comprised the Mediterranean and west African coasts and a large part of Europe to central Kazakhstan. This is a polytypical species, with 11 different known subspecies. It lives in streams, especially where the current is weak, in ponds, stagnant river branches and swamps. It is also common in brackish coastal lagoons and well adapted to artificial lakes, even of small dimensions.

Characteristics The carapace is on average 13 to 18 cm (5–7 in) long. Females are bigger and heavier. The flattened body has a smooth oval shell; the males have a slightly concave plastron and a very long tail, broadening at the base. Coloration varies from one species to another but is generally black, with a scattering of yellowish spots and lines on the carapace, legs and head.

Mating takes place in April and May, while eggs are laid from June to the end of August. The females deposit from 3 to 15 long oval eggs with pliable chalky-white shells in a small hole at most 15 cm (6 in) deep. In natural conditions, they hatch some 80 days later, but "overwintering" often occurs, whereby the fully formed young overwinter inside the eggs and emerge in the spring.

The diet is carnivorous, with an emphasis, among the very young, on small aquatic invertebrates. With growth, they graduate to almost any type of live (or fallen) prey in the water. Adults, however, supplement this with vegetation, mainly aquatic plants.

Situation Reduction in numbers over much of Europe is due principally to human interference: for centuries, the turtle has been captured for food or destroyed because it is considered harmful to fish and aquaculture. Recent causes for its dwindling populations include pollution of the water, embankment construction, control of river flow and mechanical cleaning of banks and beds—all of which prevent the turtles from carrying out their vital activities (feeding, coming ashore to bask, moving about and laying eggs). The species is protected by the Berne Convention, has priority rating under the Habitat Directive 42 1993 and is safeguarded by various national regulations.

Two or three times a season, the females of Emys orbicularis *(facing page) stray a short distance at night from the water to excavate small holes. Here, they lay their eggs and completely cover them. The death rate among the young is very high, mainly as a result of predation.*

Genetic investigation and study has made it possible to differentiate the various subspecies of the European Emys orbicularis. The removal, over the centuries, of individuals of this species from various regions for commercial purposes has not eased the problem of identification. Below, specimens of E. o. orientalis basking in the sun.

SUBSPECIES OF THE EUROPEAN POND TURTLE

According to leading experts of the species in Europe, there are two lines of descent for *Emys orbicularis*: an eastern line, comprising two groups and at least five subspecies; and a western line, with three groups and at least six more subspecies.

Eastern line
orbicularis group (Black Sea distribution) with the subspecies *E. o. orbicularis* and *E. o. colchica*.
hellenica group (eastern Mediterranean distribution) with the subspecies *E. o. hellenica*, *E. o. kurae* and *E. o. orientalis*.

Western line
luteofusca group (from central Turkey) with the subspecies *E. o. luteofusca*.
occidentalis group (from Iberian peninsula and North Africa) with the subspecies *E. o. occidentalis* and *E. o. fritzjuergenobsti*.
galloitalica group (from southern France, Italian peninsula, Corsica and Sardinia) with the subspecies *E. o. galloitalica*, *E. o. lanza* and *E. o. capolongoi*.

Taxonomists are still endeavoring to define more precisely the range of the different subspecies, which will be extremely important in the interests of their conservation.

In recent years, in fact, the European pond turtle has become the species symbol for projects relating to animals in protected areas, including the acquisition of reproductive nuclei to initiate repopulation and the reintroduction of these to populations genetically and ecologically different to those of the original native forms.

The maximum known dimension of the species is around 20 cm (8 in). Left, a large female (E. o. capolongoi) from Sardinia. Above, the overall appearance and plastron design of specimens of E. o. hellenica, from Dalmatia, and the head of an individual of E. o. galloitalica, from the Po River valley, Italy.

Spanish pond turtle
Mauremys leprosa (Schweigger, 1812)

8

Family Bataguridae.
Distribution and habitat
Spain, Portugal and southern France, North Africa from western Libya to Mauritania and south to the northern regions of Niger and southern zones of Algeria. It occupies a variety of aquatic habitats, even of limited extent, as well as artificial creations (irrigation ditches, ponds, watering holes).

Characteristics The carapace of large females is up to 20 cm (8 in) long. There is a prominent keel and a bright yellow or orange ocellus pattern in the postocular zone. The name *leprosa* derives from the sparse thickenings of the shell as a result of bacterial infections and parasitic algae.

Mating takes place in April and May, usually in water, and 6 to 12 eggs are laid in small holes excavated a few meters from the water. Incubation ranges from 70 to 90 days. The diet is essentially car-nivorous, comprising small fish, aquatic invertebrates and the dead bodies of small fish that have fallen into the water.

Situation The populations in France and eastern Spain are very localized and at risk from the modifications of habitat and the drying up of pools and ponds. The future of the species in other areas is likewise threatened by the progressive alterations to their watery habitats, and for this reason, the turtles are protected under the Berne Convention and receive conservation priority under the Habitat Directive 42/1993.

Family Bataguridae.

Distribution and habitat There are two presently recognized species of clemmids: *Mauremys rivulata* is distributed from the south of Bosnia-Herzegovina and Bulgaria to western Turkey, Israel, Syria and Lebanon (also recorded in Cyprus and Crete); *M. caspica* (Gmelin, 1774) ranges from central Turkey to Iran, Iraq, Saudi Arabia, Georgia, Azerbaijan and Turkmenistan, with two subspecies *M. m. caspica* and *M. c. ventrimaculata*. Both are common along rivers and coastal marshes.

Characteristics The length of the carapace measures from 20 cm (8 in) in *M. rivulata* and up to 23.5 cm (9¼ in) in *M. caspica*.

Males of these species are territorial and aggressive and can cause serious injury to weaker rivals or males of other species. Each female lays 3 to 6 eggs in a small chamber excavated not far from the water. They hatch after about 75 days' incubation. The diet is practically omnivorous, although small prey constitute a large part of it.

Situation The turtles are imported more or less illegally, as pets or for eating, into several European countries. Elsewhere, reg-ulations prohibit their being reared and kept in captivity.

Japanese turtle
Mauremys japonica (Temminck & Schlegel, 1835)

10

66

Family Bataguridae.

Distribution and habitat It is endemic to various Japanese islands, such as Honshu, Kyushu and Shikoku, where it inhabits streams with a sandy or muddy bottom.

Characteristics The carapace is up to 18 cm (7 in) in length. The coloration of the carapace varies from gray-green to blackish. The plastron is often completely black.

Females lay 5 to 9 eggs 2 or 3 times a year; they hatch after some 70 days. The diet of this species is omnivorous, with fish and amphibians included in the prey.

Situation It is protected at a national level; some populations are endangered by modifications of their natural habitat.

Chinese pond turtle
Chinemys reevesii (Gray, 1831)

11

Family
Bataguridae.
Distribution and habitat
Japan, southern China, Korea and Taiwan, where it has a preference for stagnant water and small streams with a sandy or muddy bottom. Although no forms of subspecies have been identified, many populations exhibit unique physical features and patterns, such as those of Japan (somewhat larger in size) and Taiwan (with more pale streaks on the neck).
Characteristics The carapace is at most 24 cm

(10 in) long; females are larger than males. The shape is elongate, with three keels, especially prominent in young specimens. Coloration is highly variable, with different shades of brown and black streaks along the keels.

After mating in spring, the females lay 4 to 9 eggs in each of 2 to 3 clutches through June and July. The hatchlings emerge after about 90 days. The diet is omnivorous: aquatic plants, insects, worms, small crustaceans and small fish.
Situation This is one of the most abundant species of those sold in shops as pets. In recent years, exports to the West from Taiwan and the cities of Southeast Asia have been stepped up considerably.

Family Testudinidae.
Distribution and habitat
Today this tortoise's range
is discontinuous and often
sparse through southern
Europe: southeastern Spain

and the Balearics, south-
ern France and Corsica,
central and southern Italy,
Sardinia and Sicily, the
coasts of Dalmatia, Herzegovina, Montenegro, Ser-

bia, Macedonia, Albania
and Greece, Romania and
Bulgaria. The Balkan pop-
ulations are separated
into the subspecies *T. h.
boettgeri* (see page 71). The
species is found in dry
coastal and inland areas,
such as established sand
dunes, scrubland, pine
woods, the Mediterranean
oak woods (including ilex
and cork), hedges around
farmland and meadows.
Characteristics The carapace is 12 to 20 cm (5–8
in) in length, but up to 23
cm (9 in) in females of
T. h. boettgeri. It is distinguished from the other
species of the genus in
having, as a rule, divided

supracaudal scutes, the tip of the tail covered with a horny spur and the color clear ocher-yellow with blackish streaks.

The tortoises become dormant at the end of October and awake in March and April. Nesting occurs in May and June. The females dig a small hole to lay 3 to 12 oval or roundish eggs with a white chalky shell, sometimes in clutches 20 days or so apart. The young hatch within 60 to 90 days, although they may overwinter in the eggs and emerge the following spring. At birth, they mea-

sure 30 to 40 mm (1–1½ in) and weigh 6 to 8 g (less than an ounce).

The diet is mainly herbivorous, comprising a variety of vegetable matter; but the young and sometimes the adults also catch small snails and other small invertebrates.

Situation Seriously threatened by modifications to their environment (especially by the extension of cereal cultivation and mechanized farming methods) and direct capture, the populations of Hermann's tortoise have for some time been protected at national

and international levels (CITES Appendix II, EEC C1, Berne Appendix B). Many organizations are also engaged in safeguarding and expanding the wild populations. In France, there is the Station d'observation de protection des tortues des Maures (SOP-TOM), based at Gonfaron; in Spain, the Asociación de Naturalistas del Sureste (ANSE) and the Comissió Medi Ambient Ajuntament de Masquefa (COMAM); and in Italy, CARAPAX, the European Centre for the Conservation of Chelonians, the WWF Lazio Delegation at Palo Laziale, Macchiagrande and the Lake Seranella Nature Reserve in Abruzzo.

It is easy to distinguish the sexes of Hermann's tortoise; the female, top right, has a more convex carapace and a flatter plastron, while the head is small and the tail barely projects and is narrow down to the base. The male, top left, has a slightly hollowed plastron and a long tail with a broad base. Left, the male of this pair is on the left.

The two subspecies of Hermann's tortoise: right, a female of Testudo hermanni hermanni; bottom, a female of Testudo h. boettgeri.

THE TWO SUBSPECIES OF HERMANN'S TORTOISE

It is relatively simple to tell the two subspecies apart as long as specimens are not the result of artificial crossbreeding.

Testudo hermanni hermanni (Gmelin, 1789)
It is of smaller size and has a rather domed shell of bright and contrasting colors, with a yellowish mark on the back of the head and two rows of parallel black stripes continuing along the length of the plastron but not to the scutes of the throat. The pectoral scutes are short in comparison with the femoral scutes.

Males are sexually mature when they measure 12 cm (5 in). The females lay 1 to 3 eggs per clutch. Many conservation proj-

Left, comparison of the ventral patterns of the two Testudo hermanni subspecies: top, three young specimens of T. h. hermanni; bottom, two adults of T. h. boettgeri. Below, much of the original distribution range of Hermann's tortoise has been irreversibly altered and turned to desert in order to accommodate widespread and intensive cultivation.

ects are in operation for this subspecies in various European countries; some include the restoration of habitats or the transfer of animals to more suitable environments (as, for example, to escape areas vulnerable to fires). It is still the object of illegal capture and has been bred successfully in numerous private establishments.

Testudo hermanni boettgeri (Mojsisovics, 1889)
This is a bigger subspecies, with the domed shell higher at the rear, the coloration more variable but not so contrasted, the black marks being less distinct; those of the plastron are discontinuous and blurred, except among some populations in Greece, where the head covers almost the whole surface of the scutes. The pectoral and femoral scutes are virtually equal in length. Males reach sexual maturity when they measure 13 cm (5 in). Each clutch contains 6 to 10 eggs. This subspecies is particularly exposed to illegal commerce and is more common among breeders; many specimens from Albania and Yugoslavia have entered Italy via the black market.

Spur-thighed tortoise
Testudo graeca (Linnaeus, 1758)

13

Family
Testudinidae.

Distribution and habitat
From southern Spain (including the Balearics) to parts of North Africa (Morocco, Algeria, Tunisia, Libya and Egypt), Sardinia, Albania, Greece, Turkey, parts of Romania and Bulgaria, Middle East and regions of southwest Asia (Iran, Iraq and Russian Caucasus).

Given its vast range, the tortoise is found in a wide variety of habitats and climatic zones, from sea level to the North African desert wadis and oases and the plateaus of Turkey and Iran, where it may occur at heights of more than 2,000 m (6,600 ft).

Characteristics The carapace averages 15 to 20 cm (6–8 in) in length, females being the larger. It differs from *T. hermanni,* with which it may share its range, in that the supracaudal scute is undivided, there is no horny tip to the tail and there are two spurs on the thighs. The active months are from March to June, with estivation during the hottest months and dormancy from late October. There are 2 to 3 clutches per year, each with 4 to 8 eggs.

The diet is herbivorous, based on grass and plants and their flowers.

Situation The most menaced populations are those of the coastal areas of Greece and along the Mediterranean shores of Turkey. The species, however, is protected from international commerce and is listed in CITES Appendix II and EEC C1. It is also protected under the Berne Convention and by national bodies (France and Italy).

SUBSPECIES OF THE SPUR-THIGHED TORTOISE

Of the existing subspecies, the following are those most readily introduced to countries in Europe.

Testudo graeca graeca
(Linnaeus, 1758)
Distribution covers southern Spain, North Africa from the Atlantic coasts of Morocco to eastern Libya, Sardinia and Sicily (where the species may have been introduced). The basic color of the carapace varies from pale yellow to olive-green or brown, each scute being dark-edged and with a black central spot. This is the subspecies with the smallest average dimensions (photograph top, and young, bottom).

Testudo graeca ibera
(Pallas, 1814)
Range includes northeastern Greece, places in Romania and Bulgaria, the more northerly Aegean islands, part of Turkish Anatolia, from the Caucasus to Azerbaijan, Iraq and Iran. Elongated, oval carapace with a broadened rear edge, less domed than the typical form. Carapace and plastron dark in color.

Testudo graeca terrestris (Forskal, 1775)
Found in southern part of Asiatic Turkey, Syria, Lebanon, western Jordan and parts of Israel. The carapace is very high and domed, with a yellow mark on the top and sides of the head.

Testudo graeca zarudnyi (Nikolskii, 1896)
Elongated and fan-shaped carapace, broader at the rear than at the front. It is found in Iran, Afghanistan and Pakistan. (Photograph in center, and young, above right.)

Marginated tortoise
Testudo marginata (Schoepff, 1792)

14

Family Testudinidae.
Distribution and habitat
It inhabits central and southern Greece and Sardinia, where it was probably introduced in historic times. Its typical habitat is evergreen scrubland in hilly, rocky zones close to agricultural land. In Sardinia, it is most frequently found in the Mediterranean scrub of the eastern coastal region.

Characteristics This is the largest species of the genus *Testudo*, reaching a maximum carapace length of 35 cm (14 in), although averaging not more than 23 cm (9 in) in males and 21 cm (8 in) in females. Some Greek populations, recently discovered, are dwarfish in size, barely measuring 15 cm (6 in). The supracaudal scute is undivided, and the carapace long and solid, flared at the rear. The carapace is black with yellow or orange areolae (which darken with age); the plastron is olive-yellow with dark triangular marks on each of the broader scutes.

Because of its almost impenetrable habitat and the seemingly low density of its populations, very little is known of its biology in the wild. Mating occurs in spring after the male has pursued and insistently attacked his partner, repeatedly bumping his shell against her and nibbling her legs. In May and June, the female digs a small cavity, where she lays 3 to 12 eggs in clutches 3 weeks apart. The young hatch in about 3 months, measuring around 40 mm (1½ in). Like the other species, it is herbivorous. **Situation** Its size, handsome appearance and relative rarity make this species a target of illegal commerce in the Mediterranean region. Fortunately, national and international laws (all chelonian species are strictly protected in Greece and Sardinia, and this one is listed in CITES Appendix II and EEC C1) have limited the damage to original populations. Nevertheless, the species is under threat from destructive summer fires.

Below, individuals of the newly identified species from Greece, Testudo weissingeri, until recently considered to be a dwarf population of Testudo marginata. Above, the typical plastron (with the dark triangular markings of the scutes) and the difference between the sexes. On the left is the male, recognizable by the visibly flared form of the carapace and the hollowing of the plastron; on the right is the female, with a much smaller tail.

Horsfield's tortoise
Testudo (= Agrionemys) horsfieldi (Gray, 1844)

15

Family Testudinidae.
Distribution and habitat
This is one of the most widely distributed tortoise species, with a range that extends from Baluchistan (Pakistan) through Iran, Afghanistan and western China to the Caspian Sea and the Volga River (where it reaches latitude 52°N). It may be seen in grassland well watered with rivulets and streams and also in areas of steppe, mountain and high plateau, though generally not above the 1,600-m (5,250-ft) mark.
Characteristics The carapace measures on average 18 to 20 cm (7–8 in), the known maximum being 22

cm (9 in); females are larger than the males. The shell is very round in shape but flattened dorsally, the color often wholly and uniformly yellow or with brownish pigmentation. The plastron is broad, with a circular black spot on each scute. The supracaudal scute is undivided. Little information is available concerning the biology of wild populations: there may be 3 clutches annually, each of 2 to 6 eggs, but as a rule, there is only 1 clutch in June.

The diet is herbivorous, but the young also feed on small invertebrates.
Situation With restrictions on commerce in various

species of the genus *Testudo* around the Mediterranean, imposed by EEC regulation 3626/1982, this species remains a prized target of illegal international traffic (CITES lists it in Appendix II).

Since the 1970s, hundreds of thousands of specimens have been caught in European Russia and imported throughout Europe, dying wretchedly either in the course of transport (crowded in their thousands into wooden crates) or through failure to adapt to habitats and diets far removed from those of their original surroundings.

Egyptian tortoise
Testudo kleinmanni (Lortet, 1883)

Family Testudinidae.

Distribution and habitat There are fairly localized populations along the coasts of North Africa, from Libya to Israel, where the species roams the western Negev. In Egypt, it is present only in the desert zones around the Nile delta, the Suez Canal and the Mediterranean shores of the Sinai Desert. It lives mainly in desert and semi-desert, with sparse, shrubby vegetation; it retires into thicker vegetation or tunnels abandoned by rodents to avoid perilous temperature extremes.

Characteristics It is a small species that reaches an average length of 10 to 15 cm (4–6 in), the females being larger than the males. The carapace is very convex and high, its color mostly sandy yellow; there may be two typical blackish triangular marks on the abdominal scutes of the plastron. The tortoises are active, especially in September and April, but spend the

hottest months in their refuges.

The Egyptian tortoise mates in March, and the females already begin to lay their eggs in late April; from then until June, they may have up to 3 clutches, each with 1 to 3 large eggs, at intervals of 20 to 30 days. The young are almost entirely yellow. The diet is herbivorous.

Situation It is very rare and under threat in various parts of its range because of destruction of its habitat and a dwindling area of bushy clumps suited to rodents that dig the tunnels in which the tortoise can take shelter.

Euphrates softshell turtle
Rafetus euphraticus (Daudin, 1802)

Family Trionychidae.
Distribution and habitat It has been reported in southern Turkey, principally in the Tigris-Euphrates basin. It is also present in Syria, Iraq, Iran and Israel. Habitats are rivers and ponds.

Characteristics The carapace measures at most 40 cm (16 in) long. The body of the adult is heavy, rounded or oval in shape, greenish with whitish or yellowish streaks, brightest in the young. The eggs are generally laid in sandy zones somewhat above the water level. It is a very active hunter, preying on invertebrates and other small aquatic creatures.
Situation Considered harmful to fish and consequently mistrusted, it is killed by local fishermen, who also destroy its eggs after they have been laid. Turkish laws to protect the species are often not enforced due to lack of personnel.

The construction of large dams along the course of the Tigris and Euphrates have probably altered its favored habitats irreversibly.

African softshell turtle
Trionyx triunguis (Forskal, 1775)

18

Family Trionychidae.
Distribution and habitat
In addition to a large part of the African continent, this species is found on the coasts of Lebanon, Syria, Israel and southern Turkey. Its inland habitats range from ponds, marshes and streams to major rivers and deep lakes and sometimes brackish water as well.

Characteristics It is one of the largest species of the *Trionyx*, with a carapace (rounded when young, oval in older adults) of more than 95 cm (38 in) in length. It is olive to dark brown, with yellowish spots (and sometimes scattered ocelli) that are more conspicuous in the young. It spends much of its life in water, even withstanding pollution (irrigation channels). The females gather in sandy zones to excavate holes close to the banks, in which they each lay 25 to 70 eggs. The diet is omnivorous, consisting mainly of small water creatures but ranging to large fish and amphibians.

AFROTROPICAL REGION

In many of the wet zones of Central Africa, little detailed study has been done of the smaller forms of wildlife. For this reason, information concerning the biology and behavior of many of the tortoises and turtles mentioned in this section is derived, for the most part, from observation of specimens raised in captivity. Preceding pages: an adult individual of Pelusios sinuatus *swimming in the company of two African otters.*

AFROTROPICAL REGION

Continental Africa and southern Sahara, Madagascar and islands of the western Indian Ocean

The Afrotropical region (formerly known as the Ethiopic), which comprises the whole of Africa south of the Sahara, the southern part of the Arabian peninsula, the islands of the western Indian Ocean and Madagascar, contains almost 50 species of Chelonia. Among the families represented are the Testudinidae (with 20 species), the Trionychidae (with 5 species) and the Pelomedusidae (with about 20 species). The presence and distribution of the different species, once determined by the extent of the preferred habitats, are today strongly linked to human activity, and many of these reptile populations have either vanished or are gravely threatened, not only because of the increasing number that are captured for food and commercial purposes but also because of the far-reaching alterations to their environment.

The majority of these species, however, have the power to adapt to change, living, according to their range, in a variety of habitats. The major deserts south of the immense Sahara itself, as well as the Ethiopian Danakil and the South African Namib and Kalahari, constitute the homes of just two

species—*Geochelone sulcata* and *Psammobates oculifera*; and the latter, together with *Kinixys natalensis*, is likewise found in the mid-desert steppes. Dry and bushy savannas are the habitats of *Geochelone pardalis*, *Malacochersus tornieri*, a few species of *Homopus* (restricted to Cape Province in South Africa), *Psammobates geometricus* and *P. tentorius*.

Various species of the genus *Pelusios* and *Pelomedusa subrufa* frequent temporary or seasonal streams and ponds; and other *Pelusios* species, several Trionychidae, notably *Trionyx triunguis*, two species of *Cycloderma* and two of

Little is known about the situation of the chelonians of this region, apart from the Testudinidae mentioned in the text. As far as the aquatic turtles are concerned, there are vast gaps in information and what data exist apply to only a few countries. Their living habitats, difficult to reach, may for the time being guarantee their safety.

Cyclanorbis are residents of large rivers and lakes.

Finally, inhabitants of rain forest, tree savanna and underbrush include other species of *Kinixys*.

Other interesting turtles and tortoises are found in Madagascar, including some of the loveliest and, unfortunately, rarest species of Testudinidae: *Geochelone radiata*, *G. yniphora*, *Pyxis arachnoides* and *P. planicauda*. One inhabitant of streams and rivers is *Erymnochelys madagascariensis*, an endemic species of the subfamily Podocnemidinae (Pelomedusidae), otherwise found only in South America.

Almost 500 km (300 miles) distant from Madagascar but still forming part of the region, the Aldabra atoll and the Seychelles archipelago are a veritable paradise for giant turtles; thousands of *Geochelone gigantea* (=*Dipsochelys dussumieri*) inhabit this small and fascinating island world.

The highly cryptic coloration, aquatic way of life and remote surroundings make it very difficult to study this family of turtles in the wild. Above, a young Pelusios; *below,* Pelomedusa subrufa.

PELOMEDUSIDAE

The present-day distribution of this family of turtles—very primitive in its anatomical and biological details, with a neck that folds sideways—ranges from South America (*see* Neotropical region) to Africa, Madagascar and certain islands of the Seychelles archipelago in the Indian Ocean.

The turtles as a rule lead a semiaquatic life and are to be found in streams, rivers and temporary or permanent pools and ponds.

Fossil remains of this group have been discovered from the Upper Cretaceous, including *Stupendemys geographicus*, one of the most formidable of freshwater tortoises ever to exist, attaining a length of 230 cm (7½ ft).

Identifying the genera of present-day Pelomedusidae

1. Hind feet with five claws → 2.

1a. Hind feet with four claws → 3.

2. Plastron with a movable hinge between the abdominal and pectoral scutes. Mesoplastra touching at plastral midline → Pelusios.

2a. Rigid plastron with no hinge between the abdominal and pectoral scutes. Fully separated mesoplastra → Pelomedusa.

3. Intergular scute totally separated from gular scutes → 4.

3a. Intergular scute not completely separated from gular scutes → Erymnochelys.

4. Presence of interorbital groove; upper jaw not hooked → Podocnemis.

4a. Absence of interorbital groove; upper jaw hooked → Peltocephalus.

The plastron of a Podocnemis.

There are two subfamilies: Podocnemidinae, with the genera *Podocnemis*, *Peltocephalus* and *Erymnochelys*; and Pelomedusidae, with the two genera *Pelomedusa* and *Pelusios*.

Erymnochelys may be considered a relict genus in biogeographical terms, inasmuch as its closest relatives live today in the opposite part of the globe, in South America. Its peculiar feature is the presence of only six neural bones in the carapace (as against seven in other Neotropical species).

Distinction between the various species of *Pelusios* is rather difficult because of the diverse interpretations among specialist authors in the classification of the genus.

The genus Erymnochelys *is the sole representative of the subfamily Podocnemidinae in the Afrotropical region. This area is the only center of distribution of the other subfamily, Pelomedusinae, and of the two genera that comprise it,* Pelusios *and* Pelomedusa.

Helmeted turtle
Pelomedusa subrufa (Lacépède, 1788)

Family Pelomedusidae.
Distribution and habitat Widespread range in tropical and subtropical Africa to South Africa. Its presence is also reported in Madagascar. Subspecies are *P. s. subrufa* (from Somalia and Sudan to Ghana and south to the Cape of Africa, in photograph below left) and *P. s. olivacea* (from Senegal, Nigeria and Cameroon to Ethiopia and Eritrea, photograph below right). The latter subspecies is regarded as the most primitive form of Pelomedusidae and is distinguished by its widely separated pectoral scutes. The species lives mainly in stagnant or temporary pools, coming ashore when it rains.

Characteristics The normal dimensions of the carapace do not exceed 20 cm (8 in). Females lay 1 clutch annually of 13 to 16 eggs, which hatch in 75 to 90 days. Carnivorous, they feed primarily on small prey.

Situation Widely distributed and quite common in most countries within its range, the species is under threat only locally, where it is caught for food; thus it is listed in CITES Appendix III at the request of several African states. It often appears as an item in the lists of European terrarium collections.

African black forest turtle

Pelusios niger (Duméril & Bibron, 1835)

Family Pelomedusidae.
Distribution and habitat It is found in west Africa, from Ghana to Cameroon, living in permanent pools on the savanna.
Characteristics The carapace is long and oval, measuring a maximum of 23 cm (9 in). The females lay a dozen or so eggs in a small chamber excavated in the grass close to the bank. The diet is carnivorous, based on the small prey of aquatic animals.
Situation Some populations are targeted for capture, often indiscriminately, for food.

African keeled mud turtle

Pelusios carinatus (Laurent, 1956)

Family Pelomedusidae.
Distribution and habitat It lives exclusively in the Congo basin in west Africa, frequenting gently flowing rivers, lakes and ponds, often at some depth.
Characteristics The carapace is elongate and oval, blackish in color, measuring about 23 cm (9 in). Because of its highly localized habitat, it is difficult to observe; as in other *Pelusios* species, the female lays 6 to 12 eggs. The diet is carnivorous.

African mud turtle
Pelusios castaneus (Schweigger, 1812)

Family Pelomedusidae.
Distribution and habitat
In west Africa, from Mauritania to Nigeria, the subspecies *P. c. castaneus* lives in the Congo, while *P. c. chapini* is found along the Congo River. They inhabit large or small pools—even temporary ones—and, should these disappear, travel some hundreds of meters toward the nearest water or spend the dry season in the mud on the bottom.

Characteristics A fairly large species, with an elongate, oval carapace up to 38 cm (15 in) long. The female deposits several clutches a year, each with 6 to 12 eggs. The diet is omnivorous, consisting mainly of water plants and large aquatic invertebrates.

Situation It is threatened locally, where captured and killed for food, but is not at present protected.

Serrated turtle
Pelusios sinuatus (Smith, 1838)

Family Pelomedusidae.
Distribution and habitat East Africa, from Somalia to Transvaal, Zululand and Natal. It lives in ponds, rivers, lakes and canals.
Characteristics The carapace may often measure up to 50 cm (20 in) in length. A good swimmer, the turtle will even venture into the central fast-flowing reaches of major rivers. Adults are sometimes observed basking on a sunny bank or log, while the young bask on floating plants. The diet is prevalently carnivorous.

Yellow-bellied mud turtle
Pelusios castanoides (Hewitt, 1931)

Family Pelomedusidae.
Distribution and habitat The subspecies *P. c. castanoides* is an inhabitant of east Africa, from Malawi and Mozambique to South Africa. The subspecies *P. c. intergularis*, however, is found in the Seychelles archipelago. The species lives in ponds and swamps.
Characteristics The elongate, oval carapace measures up to 23 cm (9 in) long. The breeding period in captivity is during the autumn months, with some 20 eggs being laid. Its biology in the wild is almost completely unknown.

East African mud turtle
Pelusios subniger (Lacépède, 1788)

Family Pelomedusidae.
Distribution and habitat
The subspecies *P. s. subniger* has been reported in Burundi and Tanzania and westward to the Congo, Zambia and Botswana, as well as Madagascar; the subspecies *P. s. parietalis* lives in Mauritius and the Seychelles. Its habitats are streams and permanent ponds, especially when stagnant.
Characteristics The carapace, measuring up to 20 cm (8 in), is oval, without keels, and brownish, as is the head and legs.

Madagascar turtle
Erymnochelys madagascariensis (Grandidier, 1867)

Family Pelomedusidae.
Distribution and habitat It is endemic to Madagascar, in a variety of wet zones.
Characteristics The carapace may measure up to 50 cm (20 in). It is an aquatic species, with an omnivorous diet that consists of water invertebrates and the shoots of aquatic plants. Eggs are laid in October and November.
Situation It has become rare as a result of being caught for food. Hence it is listed in CITES Appendix I, and educational campaigns have been launched for its protection.

TESTUDINIDAE

This family, whose fossil remains date from the Cenozoic, comprises the land tortoises, which possess a strongly convex, bony shell (except for *Malacochersus*) and dimensions that vary from those of the tiny *Homopus signatus*, at about 10 cm (4 in), to those of the giant Galápagos and Aldabra tortoises, at over 150 cm (5 ft). They have stocky, columnar legs without visible toes but with projecting claws.

They find their widest distribution and variety of form in Africa, particularly south of the Sahara; and a number of species are also present, as mentioned, in the Mediterranean basin, in southern and Southeast Asia and, in a few cases, in the Americas.

Habitats of the Testudinidae include steppes, semideserts, scrubland, savannas and, in rare instances, woods and forests; they do not appear at great heights, although species have been reported living at around 2,000 m (6,600 ft), such as *Testudo graeca* and *T. horsfieldi* in southern Asia.

These tortoises are mainly herbivorous, though some are occasionally carnivorous. Their reproductive behavior is complex, often with characteristic rituals prior to mating.

All species are seriously under threat, including *Geochelone radiata* (photograph at right), a rare species from Madagascar; for this reason, the entire group is listed and protected by CITES.

Carapace and plastron of Kinixys belliana.

Carapace and plastron of Geochelone pardalis.

Identifying the species of present-day Testudinidae

1. Carapace exhibits a posterior hinge; submarginal scutes are present between the second and third costal and between the seventh and eighth marginal scutes → Kinixys (photograph at left).
1a. Carapace lacking posterior hinge; no submarginal scutes are present → 2.
2. Plastron with a hinge → 3.
2a. Rigid plastron without a hinge → 4 (photograph at bottom).
3. Plastral hinge situated between humeral and pectoral scutes → Pyxis.
3a. Plastral hinge situated between femoral and abdominal scutes → Testudo.
4. Carapace extremely flat and depressed, with reduction in number of bones, making it fairly flexible → Malacochersus.
4a. Carapace arched, with little reduction in number of bones, thus completely rigid → 5 (photograph at left top).
5. Singular gular scute projecting strongly forward → 6.
5a. Two gular scutes, usually projecting only slightly forward → 7.
6. Small anal scute → Geochelone yniphora.
6a. Large anal scute → Chersina.
7. Jaw with medial ridge → 8.
7a. Jaw lacking medial ridge → 13.
8. Tail flattened, dorsal surface covered with enlarged scales → Acinixys (–Pyxis).
8a. Tail not flattened, dorsal surface sometimes covered with enlarged scales → 9.
9. Premaxillary bare with medial ridge; flattened forelegs → Gopherus.
9a. Premaxillary bare without ridge; forelegs columnar → 10.
10. Forefoot with four claws → Agrionemys (=Testudo).
10a. Forefoot with five claws → 11.
11. Fifth and sixth marginal scutes in contact with second pleural scute → 12.
11a. Fifth, sixth and seventh marginal scutes in contact with second pleural scute → Indotestudo.
12. Supracaudal scute divided in two → Manouria.
12a. Supracaudal scute undivided → Geochelone.
13. Carapace arched or domed dorsally; gular scutes quadrangular or of greater length than width → Psammobates.
13a. Carapace dorsally flattened, neither arched nor domed; gular scutes of greater width than length; areolae of vertebral scutes flattened → Homopus.

Giant Aldabra Tortoise
Geochelone gigantea (Schweigger, 1812)

Family
Testudinidae.
Distribution and habitat
This species is originally from Aldabra, an atoll of the Indian Ocean in the Seychelles archipelago, and has been introduced to the islands of Frégate, Mahé and Curieuse. The scientific name has undergone several changes. Recently, *Dipsochelys dussumieri* (Gray, 1831) was proposed, while the group of giant tortoises found on Mahé, the largest island of the Seychelles, was held to belong, in 1995, to the species *Dipsochelys resurrecto*. However, the name *Geochelone gigantea* now applies to all parts of the atoll.

Characteristics The carapace of the biggest specimen ever known measured 120 cm (48 in) in length. On average, the Aldabra tortoise weighs more than 180 kg (400 lb), and the length of the carapace seldom exceeds 105 cm (42 in). The nuchal plastron is unpaired. After coupling, the females, who have 2 to 3 breeding cycles a year, visit suitable sites to deposit their eggs, generally at night. Only 4 to 14 eggs are laid, and the young are born 200 days later in the midst of the rainy season. The diet is based on vegetation, grass and leaves but may also include the feces and carcasses of their own kind and other animals.

Situation Aldabra is regarded as the only ecosystem with the overwhelming presence of a herbivorous reptile (about 150,000 individuals). Since 1982, UNESCO has included this species in the list of World Heritage Sites. It is protected in CITES Appendix II.

Leopard tortoise
Geochelone pardalis (Bell, 1828)

Family Testudinidae.

Distribution and habitat It lives in east Africa from the Sahara and Ethiopia to southern Africa, with two subspecies: *G. p. pardalis,* from southwest Africa, and *G. p. babcocki,* which occupies the rest of its range (an adult of this subspecies is shown in the smaller photograph).

Leopard tortoises favor semiarid grasslands, tree savannas, dry savannas and plains. It may live at an altitude of up to 2,900 m (9,500 ft).

Characteristics The carapace is markedly convex, measuring up to 68 cm (27 in) long. Mating is preceded by lengthy pursuits and aggressive encounters, the male nipping the feet of the female and striking her with his shell.

There are multiple clutches (up to 6 a year), several weeks apart from one another. Each contains 5 to 30 eggs. The incubation period is very lengthy; the eggs take many months or even a year to hatch. Food consists of vegetation and fruit, with a preference for succulent plants and ripe fruits.

Situation It appears in CITES Appendix II and is at risk throughout almost its entire distribution range; they are hunted for food, and the eggs and young are decimated by predators.

The shells, emptied and cleaned, are used as containers or as soundboxes for various musical instruments. Despite the threat, this is still the most widely distributed African land tortoise and is often reared in captivity in the most popular tourist centers.

Radiated tortoise
Geochelone radiata (Shaw, 1802)

29

95

Family
Testudinidae.
Distribution and habitat
This species is endemic to the southernmost regions of Madagascar (Tuléar-Fort-Dauphin). It lives principally in forests consisting of the xerophytic species *Didicria* (a succulent plant similar to a cactus). It may also be found in the *Euphorbia* tree belt and in thorny scrubland.
Characteristics The carapace of large specimens can measure 40 cm (16 in) in length. It is black or brown, with a conspicuous radial pattern, the lines running from the center toward the outside.

Mating is preceded by long courtship displays on the part of the males. The females lay only 3 to 12 eggs, which incubate for 145 to 231 days. The diet is herbivorous, mostly fruit and shoots. This tortoise is very long-lived, with specimens known to be over 100 years old.
Situation It appears in CITES Appendix II, with a view to restricting commerce for terrarium collec-

tions. Populations are in fact threatened by modifications of habitat and increasing human interference, and it is the subject of several conservation and breeding projects. Reproductive nuclei are to be found in vivaria and in European and North American zoos, partly to check the heavy demand among collectors. The elegance and rarity of the species explain the much-publicized thefts from breeding centers. It is also protected under Malagasy law (no. 60-126, July 13, 1960) with the establishment of a natural reserve at Tsimanampetsotsa.

African spurred tortoise
Geochelone sulcata (Miller, 1779)

ties up to 3 meters (10 ft) long.

Characteristics This is one of the largest terrestrial species and indeed the biggest in Africa. The carapace may measure up to 80 cm (30 in) long, and it may weigh more than 60 kg (130 lb).

Annual clutches contain some 20 eggs, which are almost completely spherical. Hatchlings emerge after 60 to 100 days of natural incubation, depending on outside temperature. It is a herbivorous species that often feeds on succulent plants to absorb the water it requires; the diet also includes, apparently without trouble, the thorny branches of various shrubs.

Situation It appears in CITES Appendix II. Populations are threatened in seasons of excessive drought (sometimes rainfalls are years apart) and as a result of being captured by the inhabitants of these arid regions for food. Since 1993, a rescue project has been under way in Senegal (under the aegis of FRD Senegal and the French SOPTOM) for the collection and controlled management in breeding centers of individuals of the most threatened populations.

Family
Testudinidae.
Distribution and habitat
Central Africa, in the Sahel region, and from Eritrea to the northernmost areas of Ethiopia westward to all regions south of the Sahara and Mauritania. It is found in acacia forests and deciduous woods in arid zones. The tortoise avoids the hottest periods by digging and burying itself in cavi-

Angonoka tortoise
Geochelone yniphora (Vaillant, 1885)

Family Testudinidae.
Distribution and habitat It survives today in the wild, with just a few hundred specimens, only in the desert terrain of northwestern Madagascar, notably in the small protected zone of the Soalala/Cape Sadi region, west of Majunga. Here it is found in the bamboo forests of the coastal zones.
Characteristics The highly domed carapace measures up to 45 cm (18 in) in length; the gular scute of the plastron is in the form of a long spur. These tortoises mate after a harassing courtship by the male, who repeatedly nibbles at the legs and head of his partner to win her consent. The spur serves to impede and often to turn the female onto her carapace. During copulation, the male (as in other species of Testudinidae) lets out sharp cries. Over a year, the female may lay up to 6 clutches, with not more than 20 almost spherical eggs altogether. The species is herbivorous, feeding on grass and leaves of succulent plants.

Situation This is one of the least numerous and most endangered species in the world, with not more than 400 living specimens. Thus it is listed in CITES Appendix I, while in Madagascar, breeding and repopulation projects have been launched with the support of various international scientific bodies. Cases of poaching have been recorded—linked with the illegal international traffic in wild animals—to the direct detriment of the groups of young tortoises that have been established around the breeding centers.

South African bowsprit tortoise
Chersina angulata (Schweigger, 1812)

Family Testudinidae.

Distribution and habitat Southern Africa and Namibia from the western coastal desert to rain forests.

Characteristics The carapace measures up to 18 cm (7 in), with a long projecting gular scute, or spur. The female lays a single egg per clutch (6 to 7 a season, every 4 to 6 weeks). Incubation lasts 3 to 14 months. The diet is herbivorous.

Situation Listed in CITES Appendix II.

Speckled Cape tortoise
Homopus signatus (Schoepff, 1801)

Family Testudinidae.

Distribution and habitat It inhabits western regions of southern Africa, ranging from dry woodland to bush savanna.

Characteristics This is the smallest of all land tortoises, the males only 7 cm (3 in) and the females at most 10 cm (4 in). Little is known of it in the wild, but females lay 2 to 5 eggs at least twice a year; incubation is 100 to 130 days.

Situation It is sought for international commerce, despite its highly specialized habitats. Listed in CITES Appendix II.

Beaked Cape tortoise
Homopus areolatus (Thunberg, 1787)

Family Testudinidae.
Distribution and habitat It lives in South Africa, in the southern zones of Cape Province, notably in dry, thorny scrubland or in deciduous woods.
Characteristics With a carapace measuring at most 11.5 cm (4½ in) in length, it is, like others of the genus, one of the smallest living tortoises. The females lay 2 to 5 eggs per clutch. Incubation takes 200 to 240 days. The diet is herbivorous.
Situation Listed in CITES Appendix II.

Hinge-back tortoise
Kinixys erosa (Schweigger, 1812)

Family Testudinidae.
Distribution and habitat It ranges from Gambia to the Congo and Uganda and southward to northern Angola, in evergreen forests of very wet zones; it often ventures into small streams to find food.
Characteristics The adult carapace may exceed 30 cm (12 in). Biology as for *K. belliana* (overleaf). The diet is omnivorous.

Bell's hinge-back tortoise

Kinixys belliana (Gray, 1831)

Family Testudinidae.

Distribution and habitat The three subspecies are *K. b. nogueyi*, from Senegal to Cameroon; *K. b. belliana*, east Africa from the Congo to Kenya, Ethiopia and northeastern Somalia; and *K. b. zombensis*, from the coastal plains of east Africa, from Tanzania to Zululand. The last form has been introduced to northwestern Madagascar. The species has a preference for regions with alternate dry and rainy seasons and particularly savanna and steppe habitats.

Characteristics The carapace is e l o n g a t e, about 22 cm (9 in). It is active in early morning and evening, sheltering in holes during the heat of the day. Clutches contain 1 to 5 eggs, which hatch after a year. The diet is omnivorous.

Situation Listed in CITES Appendix II.

Home's hinge-back tortoise
Kinixys homeana (Bell, 1827)

Family Testudinidae.
Distribution and habitat West Africa, from Liberia and the Ivory Coast to the Congo. It lives in evergreen forests, in clearings with rotting vegetation, and on more open terrain but with adequate shrub cover.

Characteristics The carapace, which is typically angular and closed at the back, measures up to 22 cm (9 in) long. The females lay 2 to 5 eggs, which take 150 days to incubate. It is an omnivorous species that feeds chiefly on herbaceous plants and fruit, supplemented by small insects and land mollusks. It is particularly elusive and timid by nature.

Situation Liable to be killed by fires lit to "cleanse" zones already cleared of forest or to be caught and resold for the illegal traffic in wild animals. Despite this, protection of its populations is confined to CITES, where it is listed with others of its genus in Appendix II.

African pancake tortoise
Malacochersus tornieri (Lindholm, 1929)

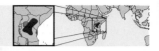

Family Testudinidae.
Distribution and habitat Tanzania and central Kenya, in arid savanna, among rocks and hills with bushes and thorny plants, at levels of 30 to 1,800 m (100–6,000 ft).
Characteristics The carapace measures up to 18 cm (7 in) and is flat and flexible. Mating takes place early in the year, and 1 egg is laid in July or August. Incubation lasts 110 to 220 days. The diet consists of vegetation and fruit.
Situation Listed in Appendix II CITES.

Flat-shelled spider tortoise
Pyxis planicauda (Grandidier, 1867)

Family Testudinidae.
Distribution and habitat West coast of Madagascar, tropical deciduous forests of Morondava and Maintirano.
Characteristics The carapace is barely 12 cm (5 in) long, flattened dorsally. Almost nothing is known of the species in the wild. The diet is herbivorous.
Situation The present state of the population is unknown, but there is a high demand from the international collectors' market because of its small size and its patterning. It is listed in Appendix II CITES.

Madagascar spider tortoise
Pyxis arachnoides (Bell, 1827)

Family
Testudinidae.
Distribution and habitat
South coast of Madagascar. There are three

subspecies:
P. a. arachnoides, *P. a. brygooi* and *P. a. oblonga*. All live in clearings of tropical deciduous forests and dry woodlands of Didieraceae and Euforbiaceae.

Characteristics The carapace, highly domed, is up to 13 cm (6 in). The female lays 1 large egg a year. The diet is herbivorous.

Situation Its populations may be under threat from excessive hunting by wild swine and from capture for food or commerce. It is listed in CITES Appendix II. The principal conservation project is that of Ampijora, known as Angonoka-Kapidoulou, initiated by the Malagasy government under the sponsorship of the Wildlife Trust and the international WWF.

Tent tortoise
Psammobates tentorius (Bell, 1828)

Family Testudinidae.
Distribution and habitat Southern Namibia and northern Cape Province. It is a highly variable species, both in the color and shape of the carapace, with three distinct subspecies: *P. t. tentorius*, *P. t. trimeni* and *P. t. verroxii*. It lives in dry and bushy woodlands and, in the savanna, sandy or rocky terrain.

Characteristics The oval carapace, with raised scutes and a radiating design, measures up to 14 cm (6 in). Females lay 1 to 3 eggs once a year, which hatch after 150 to 180 days. Herbivorous, it often supplements the diet with the feces of large mammals.

Situation Like other African land tortoises, it is threatened by the reduction of its original habitats and, in some cases, by the persistence of extremely dry conditions over several years. Listed in CITES Appendix II.

Geometric tortoise

Psammobates geometricus (Linnaeus, 1758)

Family Testudinidae.
Distribution and habitat South Africa, in a restricted area of southwestern Cape Province. Small populations survive in scrubland bordering areas of pasture and cultivated crops.
Characteristics The highly convex carapace measures up to 25 cm (10 in) in length and is dark brown or black with a yellow radiating pattern. The head and neck are dark brown or black with yellow patches. The females lay 12 to 15 eggs per clutch.

The diet is herbivorous. Isolated individuals may also be found in areas completely despoiled of vegetation; these are probably vagrants in a vain search for others of their kind.
Situation It is listed in CITES Appendix I and is one of the most endangered species in the world by reason of its dwindling habitat.

African softshell turtles

Family Trionychidae.
Distribution and habitat Africa harbors two endemic genera of Trionychidae—*Cyclanorbis* and *Cycloderma*—both represented by two species. They live in slow-flowing rivers and in marshes as well as ponds. They breed at the end of the rainy season, laying up to 20 eggs in a single clutch. They are carnivores, feeding mainly on invertebrates, fish and amphibians.

Central Africa is the home of the Nubian softshell turtle *Cyclanorbis elegans* (Gray, 1869), which has a large rounded carapace up to 60 cm (24 in) long; like the related species *C. senegalensis*, it is often caught by local fishermen for food. In Malawi, Mozambique and Tanzania lives the Zambezi softshell turtle *Cycloderma frenatum* (Peters, 1854), illustrated below. It has an oval carapace measuring up to 56 cm (22 in) long (a centimeter or so less in the related species *C. aubryi*) and frequents ponds in the rain forests of southeastern Africa.

ORIENTAL REGION

ORIENTAL REGION

India, Indochinese Peninsula, Malaysia, Philippines, Sonda Islands

If we had a mind to plan the ideal journey to study as many species of turtles and tortoises in their wild habitats covering the fewest miles, we could do no better than visit those countries facing the Bay of Bengal or lying under the shadow of the Himalayas—northeastern India, Nepal, Bangladesh and Myanmar. This is the area watered jointly by the Ganges and Brahmaputra Rivers and, much farther to the southeast, by the Irrawaddy. These immense river basins nurture innumerable aquatic sites that supplement the vast zones of artificial swampland constituted by the cultivation of rice. These conditions are ideal for many species of Bataguridae and Trionychidae. Here are found the softshell "proboscis" turtles of the genus *Chitra*, the *Nilssonia*

Previous spread, a specimen of Cistoclemmys flavomarginata on the outskirts of a rice paddy in southern China.

species and the gigantic *Aspideretes;* on the banks and among the floating plants are turtles of the genera *Kachuga* and *Lissemys;* in the streams and neighboring marshes are specimens of *Geoclemys, Hardella, Heosemys* and *Melanochelys;* and on land, well protected by their box-like shell, are individuals of *Cuora amboinensis.*

The Oriental region, however, also takes in the rest of India, Sri Lanka, Indochina, Indonesia, a large part of China, Hainan and Taiwan, the Philippines and the Sonda Islands. This huge region represents, at least in theory, a paradise for many aquatic and semiaquatic species (of the genera *Platysternon, Cuora, Siebenrockiella, Sacalia, Pyxidea, Orlitia, Chinemys* and *Mauremys*); others almost completely independent of water (*Geoemyda* and *Cistoclemmys*); and yet others entirely terrestrial (*Manouria, Indotestudo* and *Geochelone*). Unfortunately, here, the turtles and tortoises are threatened by the destruction of their habitats and by their capture for food and commerce, ending up in terrariums and as ingredients for traditional medicines. Bearing the brunt of this trade are the species of largest size, such as certain Trionychidae (*Aspideretes, Palea steindachneri, Pelochelys bibroni*) and several Bataguridae (*Batagur* and *Callagur*), as well as those with the most beautiful designs (*Geoemyda, Heosemys, Ocadia* and *Cuora*) or of particular rarity (*Manouria impressa* and *Chitra chitra*).

In the temples of Nepal, India and Thailand, it is not uncommon to find species such as *Indotestudo elongata, Melanochelys tricarinata* and *Kachuga tecta* being reared as incarnations of the god Vishnu or in gratitude to Buddha.

In southern China and Indochina, it is still possible to discover new species. In recent years, descriptions have been circulated of several interesting members of the genus *Cuora* (*C. pani, C. mccordi* and *C. aurocapitata*), *Mauremys iversoni, Ocadia philippeni* and *Sacalia pseudocephala,* some of which, in terms of biological detail, remain almost an unknown quantity.

Facing page, a watercourse in the tropical jungle of Thailand and rice paddies. Above, a coastal swamp zone. This region, depending on one's point of view, is either a paradise or hell for the turtles that live here. The ranges of the dozens of species endemic to the region are becoming increasingly confined, and their populations are dwindling in numbers. Meanwhile, human pressure grows all the time.

TRIONYCHIDAE

These chelonians characteristically possess a carapace that contains few, if any, bones and is covered with leathery skin instead of horny scales. Because of this peculiarity, the reptiles are known as softshell turtles.

Markedly aquatic and expert swimmers, the turtles typically have the toes of their feet joined by broad webbing to form flippers. The tip of the snout is long, almost tubular, and the nostrils are situated at the very end so that they can stay completely submerged and able to breathe by keeping only the tip of the nose out of the water. In some cases, breathing is further assisted by vascular tissue in the cloaca and throat.

These turtles are elusive and skilled in fleeing from predators, but their strong jaws can also inflict injury. Sexual dimorphism is often conspicuous: females are more likely to change their coloration and patterning over the years, though the tone remains uniformly dark, while males have a long tail, thicker at the base. They are distributed from the Mediterranean basin (*Trionyx triunguis*) to the whole of Africa (*Cyclanorbis, Trionyx, Cycloderma*) and to southern and eastern Asia, the Philippines, Sumatra and New Guinea (*Lissemys, Amyda, Aspideretes, Chitra, Dogania, Nilssonia, Rafetus, Palea, Pelochelys, Pelodiscus*) and as far as North America (*Apalone*).

All these turtles are primarily carnivorous and active predators, particularly agile in the water and readily able to catch fish and other small invertebrates. The status of the majority of the species is little known, because their wide diffusion and elusive habits make observation and counting difficult. The large species are mercilessly hunted for their flesh or because they allegedly cause damage; certain small and handsome species are also at risk from the international pet trade (*Lissemys, Apalone*). Only two species, nevertheless, are believed to be in danger of extinction (*Aspideretes nigricans* and *Chitra chitra*).

Above, Apalone spinifera *and* Apalone ferox. *Below, the small plastron of* Apalone spinifera. *These turtles, unmistakable because of their leathery carapace and snout elongated into a proboscis, are very agile and perfectly adapted to life in water. Their aggressive nature compensates for the poor protection afforded by the soft shell.*

Identifying the species of present-day Trionychidae

1. Six or more callosities present on surface of plastron; femoral folds of skin (flaps) on sides of plastron → Subfamily Cyclanorbinae.
1a. Four or five callosities present on surface of plastron; no folds of skin on sides of plastron → Subfamily Trionychinae.
2. Peripheral bones in shell; species from India, Bangladesh and Burma → Lissemys.
2a. No peripheral bones in shell → 3.
3. Neural bones form a continuous series; postorbital arch wider than maximum diameter of orbit. In Africa → Cycloderma.
3a. Series of neural bones discontinuous; postorbital arch narrower than maximum diameter of orbit. In Africa → Cyclanorbis.
4. Proboscis longer than maximum diameter of orbit → 5.
4a. Proboscis shorter than maximum diameter of orbit →Pelochelys.
5. Postorbital arch much larger than maximum diameter of orbit; grinding surface of jaws sharp and narrow → Chitra.
5a. Postorbital arch much shorter than maximum diameter of orbit; grinding surface of jaws broad and flattened → 6.
6. Long anterior preplastral extensions → 7.
6a. Short- or medium-size anterior preplastral extensions → 8.
7. All eight costal bones touch in middle → Dogania.
7a. Seventh and eighth pair of costal bones linked to neural bones → 9.
8. Seven plastral callosities present → Pelodiscus.
8a. Four or five plastral callosities present → 10.
9. Only four plastral callosities present; length of nuchal bone one-third of the width → Palea.
9a. Five plastral callosities; length of nuchal bone at least three times the width → Amyda.
10. Medium-size anterior preplastral extension → Aspideretes.
10a. Short anterior preplastral extension → 11.
11. Length of nuchal bone less than three times the width → Nilssonia.
11a. Width of nuchal bone three or more times the length → 12.
12. Eighth pair of costal bones complete, not reduced → Trionyx.
12a. Eighth pair of costal bones reduced or absent → 13.
13. Only two callosities on surface of plastron → Rafetus.
13a. Four or five callosities on surface of plastron → Apalone.

Left to right and top to bottom: skulls of Cyclanorbis spp. and Cycloderma spp. seen from the side (a-b); backs of Pelochelys spp. and of Chitra (c-d); belly of Apalone spp. (e).

c

d

e

a

b

Indian flap-shell turtle
Lissemys punctata (Lacépède, 1788)

42

Family Trionychidae. **Distribution and habitat** India, Pakistan, Sikkim, Nepal, Bangladesh, Sri Lanka and Myanmar; range includes Indus and Ganges Rivers and their tributaries. There are two distinct subspecies: *L. p. punctata* in the Indian peninsula and Sri Lanka, and *L. p. andersoni* in the remainder of the range. *L. p. scutata*, formerly considered another subspecies, is nowadays regarded as a distinct species. All of them prefer stagnant water or slow-flowing tracts of rivers where the bottom is muddy, with plenty of aquatic plants.

Characteristics It is the most primitive genus of the Trionychidae, typically with peripheral bones in the rear part of the carapace, which may measure up to 28 cm (11 in); the carapace varies from brown to green, with a cream-colored plastron. The species has only three claws on each foot. There are seven dark, grainy peripheral callosities on the plastron; the rest of the skin is soft, with two flexible, protruding flaps near the hind legs.

Females lay 2 to 14 eggs several times a year, in a hole dug a short distance from the water. The turtles are omnivorous and can catch fish and amphibians. **Situation** The subspecies *L. p. punctata* is protected in CITES Appendix I. With its design of yellow spots on head and carapace, it is gravely endangered by animal commerce. In some places, it is hunted for its meat. Various population census and conservation projects have been launched.

Asiatic softshell turtle

Amyda cartilaginea (Beddaert, 1770)

Family Trionychidae.
Distribution and habitat From southern Myanmar to the Malaysian peninsula, Indonesia. It inhabits ponds, swamps and marshes near major rivers.
Characteristics Oval olive-colored carapace up to 70 cm (28 in) long. Females annually lay 3 to 4 clutches of 3 to 6 eggs, which hatch after more than 130 days. The carnivorous diet comprises aquatic invertebrates, fish and amphibians.
Situation Killed for food; breeding sites are endangered by extraction of sand.

Chinese softshell turtle

Pelodiscus sinensis (Wiegmann, 1835)

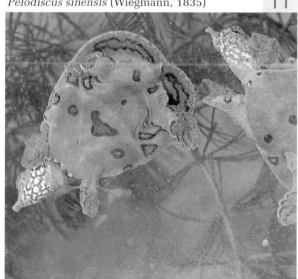

Family Trionychidae.
Distribution and habitat Widely diffused in central and southern China, northern Vietnam, islands of Hainan and Taiwan, Korea and Japan. Some populations also live in the extreme southeastern regions of Russia (basins of the Amur and Ussuri). It inhabits all types of fresh water.
Characteristics The oval carapace has a marginal crest and measures up to 25 cm (10 in). Females lay 20 to 30 eggs 3 or 4 times a year. Carnivorous, it prefers fish, crustaceans and mollusks.

Black softshell turtle
Aspideretes nigricans (Anderson, 1875)

Family Trionychidae.

Distribution and habitat This rare species is restricted to artificial basins at Nasirabad, near Chittagong, Bangladesh.

Characteristics The flat carapace measures up to 80 cm (32 in). The turtle comes ashore to lay eggs and to bask. An excellent swimmer, it catches fish, mollusks and other aquatic invertebrates.

Situation Endangered by capture for food, it is listed in CITES Appendix I. A program of management and protection has been launched.

Ganges softshell turtle
Aspideretes gangeticus (Cuvier, 1825)

Family Trionychidae.

Distribution and habitat Basins of the rivers Ganges, Indus and Mahanadi and in Afghanistan, Pakistan, India, Bangladesh and southern Nepal. It lives in the flowing water of large rivers and canals, with a preference for those with a muddy or sandy bottom.

Characteristics The oval or rounded carapace is up to 70 cm (28 in) long. There are three claws on each of the hind and forefeet. Hardly perceptible callosities are present on the plastron. The diet is omnivorous, based on fish, amphibians, mollusks and aquatic plants.

Situation Listed in CITES Appendix I, it is the subject of a program for breeding in captivity and reintroduction to various sites in the Ganges basin.

Big-headed turtle

Platysternon megacephalum (Gray, 1831)

PLATYSTERNIDAE

Because of certain anatomical features, this family, represented by a single living species (*Platysternon megacephalum*), has often been grouped together with the Chelydridae, but studies of chromosomes have revealed a closer phyletic relationship to the Bataguridae.

The most striking aspect of this turtle is the large triangular head (with a sturdy skull)—often half the length of the carapace—covered with horny plates on back and sides. The well-developed jaws are covered with a horny layer that terminates in a hook.

Family Platysternidae.

Distribution and habitat With five subspecies (*P. m. megacephalum, P. m. peguense, P. m. vogeli, P. m. tristernalis* and *P. m. shiui*), it is found from southern and eastern China to Vietnam, Laos, Cambodia, Thailand and Myanmar. It is an inhabitant of mountain streams with stony beds and concealment.

Characteristics The head is large, almost half the width of the carapace, which is barely 20 cm (8 in). The skull (illustrated at upper right) is covered with broad, thick, horny layers. The turtle is poorly adapted for swimming and moves around by tramping the bottom or clambering over rocks (it can climb bushes and trees). Females lay 1 to 2 elliptical eggs once a year.

It leads a nocturnal life, leaving its shelter to catch its prey (invertebrates and small fish). It bites in fury or opens its hooked jaws wide to frighten off aggressors.

Situation It is endangered by reason of its typical habitat and low breeding rate; IUCN initiated an action plan in 1991 to check on its status and need for protection.

BATAGURIDAE

Of all living chelonians, the Old World pond turtles constitute the group with the largest number of genera (23) and species (about 60), and new species or taxonomic modifications are virtually the order of the day.

Their area of distribution extends from southern Europe and North Africa (with some species of *Mauremys*) to Southeast Asia, Indonesia, the Philippines and Japan; but they include one genus, *Rhinoclemmys*, from Central and South America. They are distinguished from the Emydidae—the family most closely related phyletically and morphologically and of which it was until recently considered a subfamily—by certain anatomical characteristics. The angular bone of the lower jaw is completely or partially separated from Meckel's cartilage by a prearticular bone; the basioccipital bone is large, with a lateral growth that forms the floor of the tympanic cavity; finally, there is a single joint between the fifth and sixth cervical vertebrae. In comparison with other very primitive families, the Bataguridae lack inframarginal and intergular scutes as well as mesoplastral bones. Dimensions vary from around 10 cm (4 in) of some *Cuora* to almost 90 cm (3 ft) in *Callagur* and *Batagur*. They are eclectic in their way of life and in their

Above, head of Cuora amboinensis. *Bottom right, head of* Orlitia borneensis. *Below, plastron of* Cuora mccordi. *The variety of forms, sizes and patterns makes this large family unique; and the overall picture has benefited greatly in recent years from observations of the many species in their natural habitats.*

The serrated appearance of the rear part of the carapace of Geoemyda spengleri, *left, and of* Pyxidea mouhotii, *below.*

choice of habitat: they live in water that may be either stagnant or fast-flowing, in ponds and lagoons, in rivers and swamps; certain species may wander far from water, while others lead a life that is almost wholly terrestrial (such as *Rhinoclemmys* and *Heosemys*)—only *Callagur borneoensis* frequents brackish water.

The species living in eastern Asia and southern China are widely hunted and caught for eating and for collection in terrariums. Indeed, the family comprises groups such as *Cuora*, *Chinemys* and *Cyclemys*, which are very popular in the pet shops of the West.

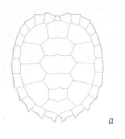

a

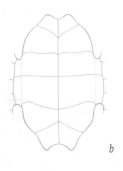

b

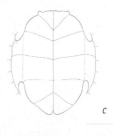

c

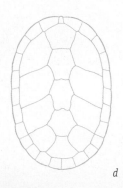

d

Identifying the genera of present-day Bataguridae

1. *Plastron with hinge moving freely between pectoral and abdominal scutes → 2.*
1a. *Rigid plastron without a hinge or a partially movable bridge only in females → 5.*
2. *Posterior edge of carapace unserrated; large plastral lobes, capable of closing the shell completely → Cuora.*
2a. *Posterior edge of carapace serrated; narrow plastral lobes, incapable of closing the shell completely → 3.*
3. *Five vertebral scutes present → 4.*
3a. *Six or seven vertebral scutes present → Notochelys (a).*
4. *Vertebral zone of carapace much flattened; intergular seam shorter than seam between humeral scutes → Pyxidea (b).*
4a. *Vertebral zone of carapace barely flattened; intergular hinge longer than hinge between humeral scutes → Cyclemys (c).*
5. *Grinding surface of jaw broad, at least at rear → 6.*
5a. *Grinding surface of jaw narrow → 17.*
6. *Grinding surface of jaw very broad; when present, the medial crest terminates in a cusp → 7.*
6a. *Grinding surface of jaw fairly broad, without a frontal cusp → 9.*
7. *Grinding surface of jaw with barely perceptible or no medial crest → Geoclemys.*
7a. *Grinding surface of jaw with perceptible medial crest → 8.*

8. *Yellow plastron without marks; pleural scutes usually with light-colored ocelli; choanae open at level of orbit → Morenia.*
8a. *Plastron with dark mark above each scute; pleural scutes without ocelli; choanae open behind orbits → Hardella.*
9. *Grinding surface of jaw broad at back but narrow in middle → 10.*
9a. *Grinding surface of jaw broad throughout length → 11.*
10. *Grinding surface of jaw with medial crest; second vertebral scute mushroom-shaped with base pointing to rear; fourth pleural scute small → Orlitia (d).*
10a. *Grinding surface of jaw without medial crest; second vertebral scute not mushroom-shaped; fourth pleural scute hardly smaller than others → Siebenrockiella (e).*
11. *Grinding surface of jaw with single medial crest; five claws on forefeet → 12.*
11a. *Grinding surface of jaw with two crests; four claws on forefeet → Batagur (f).*
12. *Crest on grinding surface of jaw pointed and prominent → 13 (g).*
12a. *Crest on grinding surface of jaw small or indistinct → 15 (h).*
13. *Length of fourth vertebral scute greater than width → Kachuga (n).*
13a. *Width of fourth vertebral scute greater than length → 14 (m).*

14. *Neck with many yellow, black-bordered streaks* → Ocadia *(i).*
14a. *Neck without streaks* → Callagur.
15. *Crest on grinding surface of jaw present but small or indistinct* → 16.
15a. *No crest on grinding surface of jaw* → Chinemys *(p).*
16. *Carapace serrated at back, with single longitudinal keel* → Hieremys.
16a. *Carapace not serrated at back (but with a single medial depression), with three longitudinal keels* → Malayemys.
17. *Carapace with single longitudinal keel* → 18.
17a. *Carapace with three longitudinal keels* → 19.
18. *One or two pairs of colored ocelli at back of head; Southeast Asia* → Sacalia.
18a. *No colored ocelli at back of head; Neoarctic and Neotropical regions* → Rhinoclemmys.
19. *Carapace unserrated or slightly serrated at rear* → 20.
19a. *Carapace strongly serrated at rear* → 22.
20. *Dorsal and lateral keels of carapace low, but pronounced in adults* → Melanochelys.
20a. *Dorsal and lateral keels of carapace barely evident in adults* → 21.
21. *Plastral spurs well developed* → Annamemys.
21a. *Average development of plastral spurs* → Mauremys.
22. *Intergular hinge shorter than medial hinges separating plastral scutes* → Geoemyda.

22a. *Intergular hinge not shorter than medial hinge separating plastral scutes* → Heosemys.

f

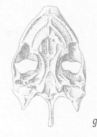

g

h

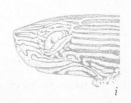

i

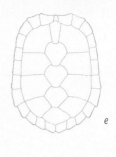

e

l

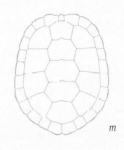

m

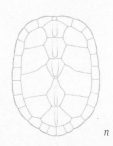

n

Chinese yellow-edged box turtle
Cistoclemmys flavomarginata (Gray, 1863)

47

120

Family Bataguridae.
Distribution and habitat In a number of places, from southern, central and eastern China to Taiwan. It lives in ponds and rice paddies and in forest streams.

Characteristics The shell is highly arched, with a yellow stripe running lengthways along the vertebral zone. The carapace measures up to 17 cm (7 in) long. The female lays 2

to 3 eggs per clutch 2 or 3 times in June and July.

The tortoise leads a semiaquatic life, remaining for long periods on land to bask and find food, which consists mainly of small invertebrates, ripe fruit and herbaceous plants. It also catches small fish in the water.

Situation Several populations are under threat from being captured for intensive breeding centers (i.e., in Taiwan); the small individuals bred in captivity are exported to many Western countries to stock the pet trade.

Indochinese box turtle

Cistoclemmys galbinifrons (Bourret, 1939)

Family Bataguridae.
Distribution and habitat Northern zone of Vietnam, in the Gulf of Ton-kin, Annam and also the island of Hainan. There are three sub-species. *C. g. galbinifrons*, *C. g. serrata* and *C. g. bouretti*. They often stray some distance from the water, leading an almost wholly terrestrial life, frequenting the underbrush of bushy and forested zones in mountainous terrain.

Characteristics The carapace is up to 19 cm (8 in) long and dark brown with three paler stripes.

It uses a passive defensive tactic when confronted by aggressors, retreating into its shell and closing the movable parts of the plastron. Little is known of its habits, but it is carnivorous, with a preference for small invertebrates.

Malaysian box turtle
Cuora amboinensis (Daudin, 1802)

Distribution and habitat It is widely distributed in Southeast Asia, including Bangladesh, Assam, Myanmar, Thailand, Cambodia, Vietnam, Malaysia, Indonesia, the Philippines and Japan.

Several forms have been described but are not currently recognized as subspecies.

It lives in small pools of stagnant water but also in swamps and rice paddies.

Characteristics As a rule, the dark green or black carapace is highly arched, measuring up to 20 cm (8 in) long. Several weeks after copulation, which takes place in shallow water, the female lays 2 to 3 eggs, with 3 to 4 clutches a year. The eggs are quite long and hatch after about 90 days.

The diet is vegetarian, based on aquatic plants and other grasses.

Situation This is one of the most popular species for collectors, and thousands of.young are exported annually to suitable breeding farms in the Philippines. To ensure breeding success, new specimens are captured continuously from wild populations, often decimating the groups irreversibly.

Yellow-headed box turtle
Cuora aurocapitata (Luo & Zong, 1988)

50

Family Bataguridae.
Distribution and habitat Southern part of Anhui province in China. It lives in streams, in zones with plenty of vegetation.
Characteristics It is a small species with a carapace up to only 14 cm (6 in) long. Almost nothing is known of its life habits.
Situation The species became so rare only a few years after its discovery, which suggests that the majority were caught for breeding and stocking wholesalers in the wild animal trade.

123

McCord's box turtle
Cuora mccordi (Ernst, 1988)

51

Family Bataguridae.
Distribution and habitat Reported only in Yunnan province and in the Guangxi Zhuang region. It lives in forest streams.
Characteristics The carapace, elliptical and domed, measures up to 14 cm (6 in). Its life habits in the wild are almost unknown.

Pan's box turtle
Cuora pani (Song, 1984)

52

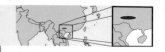

Family Bataguridae.
Distribution and habitat Discovered in recent years in southern Shaanxi and Yunnan, in China, where it lives in small streams with abundant vegetation.
Characteristics The elongate, slightly arched carapace measures up to 16 cm (6 in). Little is known about its life habits in the wild, but it is probably omnivorous, feeding mainly on aquatic plants.
Situation Only recently discovered, it has become much sought after for international trade.

Chinese three-striped box turtle
Cuora trifasciata (Bell, 1825)

53

Family Bataguridae.
Distribution and habitat It is found in several provinces of southern China and the more northerly regions of Vietnam. It favors mountain streams and ponds, often straying some way from water in search of food and warmth.
Characteristics The carapace, slightly arched and long, is at most 20 cm (8 in). There are 2 to 3 clutches a season. The diet is carnivorous, mainly small invertebrates and fish.
Situation The status of this elusive and timid species in the wild is not known.

Chinese red-necked pond turtle

Chinemys kwangtungensis (Pope, 1934)

Family Bataguridae.

Distribution and habitat From southern China, in Kwangtung province, to northern regions of Vietnam. It inhabits mountain streams at heights normally of not over 400 m (1,300 ft).

Characteristics The long and slightly arched carapace measures up to 20 cm (8 in) and has a quite pronounced keel down the middle. The diet is omnivorous. Little is yet known about its lifestyle.

Chinese big-headed pond turtle

Chinemys megalocephala (Fang, 1934)

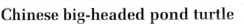

Family Bataguridae.

Distribution and habitat It is found only in the Nanking region in China, usually in ponds and streams in hilly and mountainous areas.

Characteristics The dark carapace measures up to 23 cm (9 in) long. Not much is known of its life in the wild. The diet is omnivorous, prevalently small aquatic invertebrates.

Asian leaf turtle
Cyclemys dentata (Gray, 1831)

Family Bataguridae.
Distribution and habitat From Yunnan and Guanaxi in China and from eastern India to Indochina, the Malaysian peninsula and Indonesia to Bali, Borneo and the Philippines. It lives in streams with an abundance of aquatic vegetation.
Characteristics The carapace is up to 24 cm (10 in). The female lays 2 to 3 large eggs 3 to 4 times a year. Omnivorous.

Stripe-necked leaf turtle
Cyclemys tcheponensis (Bourret, 1939)

57

Family Bataguridae.
Distribution and habitat It is a species from Vietnam, Laos, Cambodia and parts of Thailand, living in mountain streams and often spending long periods on land, even at some distance from water.
Characteristics The carapace, very long in adults, measures up to 22 cm (9 in). The female lays 10 to 15 eggs each season. The diet is omnivorous, comprising mainly aquatic plants, larvae and insects.

Black-breasted leaf turtle
Geoemyda spengleri (Gmelin, 1789)

58

Family Bataguridae. **Distribution and habitat** Southern China and the whole of Vietnam. Terrestrial, it strays some way from its streams, usu- ally situated in mountain forests. A close relative, *G. japonica*, lives in small numbers in Japan.

Characteristics It is a species of small size, not more than 13 cm (5 in) long, with a characteristi- cally elongated carapace with pointed marginal plates. The diet is omnivo- rous, principally based on insects and their larvae and ripe fruit.

Situation It is sought after by terrarium collectors for its interesting shape, its notable vitality and its capacity for adaptation. For this reason, it has become a rare species in many of its native habitats.

Asian yellow pond turtle
Mauremys mutica (Cantor, 1842)

Family Bataguridae.

Distribution and habitat Eastern and southern China, northern Vietnam and islands of Hainan and Taiwan. Two subspecies are *M. m. mutica* and *M. m. kami*. It frequents stagnant or slow-flowing low-altitude water bodies.

Characteristics The carapace measures up to 20 cm (8 in). Single-keeled forms are almost black in color; three-keeled forms are brownish yellow or brown with dark seams. The female lays several clutches a year of at most 12 eggs, which hatch in 90 days. The diet is carnivorous, consisting of small fish.

Chinese stripe-necked turtle
Ocadia sinensis (Gray, 1834)

60

Family Bataguridae.

Distribution and habitat The range of this species includes much of eastern and southern China, northern Vietnam and the islands of Hainan and Taiwan. It lives in stagnant or slow-flowing water with a sandy or muddy bed.

Characteristics The elongated carapace has three conspicuous keels and is up to 24 cm (10 in) long. The female lays 2 to 3 eggs, with 2 to 3 clutches a year. The diet is herbivorous, chiefly aquatic plants.

Situation An endangered species, captured indiscriminately for commerce.

Crowned river turtle
Hardella thurjii (Gray, 1831)

Family Bataguridae.
Distribution and habitat
Localized in Bangladesh and Pakistan, in the basins of the Indus, Brahmaputra and Ganges Rivers. Two subspecies are classified: *H. t. thurji* and *H. t. indi.* It has been sighted in many types of wet zones but

is most often found in and around slow-flowing streams with muddy beds and plenty of vegetation.
Characteristics The dimensions are linked to gender, the females measuring up to 54 cm (22 in) and the males only 18 cm (7 in). The diet is based principally on grasses and aquatic plants. It basks by floating lazily on the water surface.
Situation In many areas, it is already quite rare because of being hunted and because of human interference with its habitats in an ever-increasing quest for open space.

Spotted pond turtle

Geoclemys hamiltonii (Gray, 1831)

62

Family Bataguridae.

Distribution and habitat Northern India, Assam, southern Pakistan and Bangladesh, along the tributaries of the Indus and Ganges Rivers. It is most often observed in streams with abundant water vegetation.

Characteristics The long domed carapace, with three keels, measures up to 35 cm (14 in). The diet is carnivorous, comprising mainly small aquatic invertebrates.

Situation The distribution fragmented and the populations small, it is considered at risk.

Giant Asian pond turtle

Heosemys grandis (Gray, 1860)

63

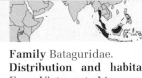

Family Bataguridae.

Distribution and habitat From Vietnam to Myanmar and the Malaysian peninsula. It inhabits running water of all types, from sea level to hilly zones.

Characteristics This is one of the largest hard-shelled, semiaquatic turtles in Asia, measuring up to 44 cm (18 in) in length. Herbivorous, it feeds on aquatic plants and algae.

Situation It is possible to see it in pools and ponds in and outside the Tortoise Temple of Bangkok, in Thailand. It is hunted for food.

Spiny turtle
Heosemys spinosa (Gray, 1831)

Family Bataguridae.
Distribution and habitat Its ideal surroundings are in Thailand, Malaysia, Sumatra and Borneo. It lives in or near streams, in wooded and forested hill and mountain regions.

Characteristics The carapace, up to 22 cm (9 in) long, is notable for the spiny projections on the edges of the pleural plates, the rear edge of each vertebral plate and each marginal plate (much more conspicuous in very young specimens). The female lays 2 to 3 large eggs a season. It is a herbivorous and frugivorous species.

Situation This species is much hunted for its unusual appearance and patterning and is widely bred in Thailand for commerce.

Red-crowned roofed turtle
Kachuga kachuga (Gray, 1831)

133

Family Bataguridae.

Distribution and habitat It is found in much of the Ganges basin from Nepal to Bangladesh, India and Myanmar, principally in deep running water, always a good distance from the banks and diving at the first sign of danger.

Characteristics The carapace, less domed than that of other related species, may measure up to 50 cm (20 in). The female's head has blue-green tints and red at the back; the male's head is red with blue-gray at the sides.

The females lay 20 to 25 long oval eggs, coming ashore at dusk and digging small holes in the bank to deposit their eggs as rapidly as possible.

It is an omnivorous species that, despite its size, moves fast in water. Although its food consists mainly of aquatic plants, it also manages to catch small fish and amphibians.

Situation It is threatened locally by being caught directly for food, especially in the Ganges basin. Larger individuals are caught in their habitats by fishermen with baited hooks and are either eaten directly or transported alive to the nearest market for sale. Protection under Indian law (Indian Wildlife Protection Act of 1972) has helped to check this traffic, and the species is recovering its numbers in other places. Construction of dams along the course of the Ganges has nevertheless resulted, in some cases (e.g., in Farakka), in their being even more gravely endangered. Indeed, flooding has destroyed all their egg-laying sites and also affected the availability of prey.

Brown roofed turtle
Kachuga smithi (Gray, 1863)

Family Bataguridae.
Distribution and habitat Basins of the Indus, Brahmaputra and Ganges Rivers, in Pakistan, India and Bangladesh. The two known subspecies are *K. s. smithi* and *K. s. pallidipes*. Habitats are large and small rivers and bodies of water associated with them.
Characteristics A species of average dimensions, up to 24 cm (10 in) long. It is very timid and elusive, taking refuge in water at the first sign of danger. The female lays 4 to 8 eggs at a time. Omnivorous.

134

Indian tent turtle
Kachuga tentoria (Gray, 1834)

Family Bataguridae.
Distribution and habitat The entire Indian peninsula and Bangladesh. It lives in all types of flowing water and pools. The three known subspecies are *K. t. tentoria*, *K. t. circumdata* and *K. t. flaviventer*.
Characteristics The carapace is strongly arched and elliptical, measuring up to 27 cm (11 in). The female lays 4 to 8 eggs at a time. The diet is omnivorous.
Situation The species is under threat from capture for food and for commerce.

Indian roofed turtle
Kachuga tecta (Gray, 1831)

Family Bataguridae.
Distribution and habitat Basins of Indus, Ganges and Brahmaputra Rivers, in Pakistan, India and Bangladesh. It is common in moderate-flowing rivers and streams but is also found in ponds, pools and artificial lakes.
Characteristics The carapace measures up to 25 cm (10 in) and is strongly arched, with a prominent central keel. Herbivorous.
Situation Listed in CITES Appendix I, with a view to limiting its capture for commercial purposes.

ORIENTAL REGION

135

Malaysian snail-eating turtle
Malayemys subtrijuga (Schlegel & Müller, 1844)

Family Bataguridae.
Distribution and habitat Vietnam, Cambodia, Thailand, Java and Malaysia. It inhabits pools and ponds with a muddy bottom and a fair provision of aquatic vegetation.
Characteristics The carapace may measure up to 20 cm (8 in) in length. Food consists ideally of snails and other water or land gastropods but also of other invertebrates.
Situation It is caught in the wild for commercial purposes (exported in their hundreds from Vietnam to Europe).

Indian black turtle

Melanochelys trijuga (Schweigger, 1812)

Family Bataguridae.
Distribution and habitat India, Bangladesh, Myanmar, Sri Lanka, Maldives and the Chagos Islands. Six subspecies are described: *M. t. trijuga*, *M. t. thermalis*, *M. t. edeniana*, *M. t. coronata*, *M. t. indopeninsularis* and *M. t. parkeri*. It is found in clear, running water, from which it may nevertheless stray for long periods.
Characteristics It measures up to about 40 cm (16 in). The female lays clutches of 3 to 8 eggs several times a year. Herbivorous, it feeds on aquatic plants.

Burmese eyed turtle

Morenia ocellata
(Dumeril & Bibron, 1835)

Family Bataguridae.
Distribution and habitat It lives in Myanmar, in permanent or seasonal ponds and pools. A second species of the genus, *M. petersi*, is found in northern India and Bangladesh.
Characteristics The carapace measures up to 21 cm (8 in), that of the female being bigger, and is olive or brownish black with yellow ocelli on the marginal and vertebral scutes, edged with black and with a central brown spot (additionally with yellowish stripes in *M. petersi*). Markedly aquatic, it is an omnivore, feeding on various types of grass and small invertebrates.
Situation Listed in CITES Appendix I to restrict its capture for food and collections.

Malaysian flat-shelled turtle

Notochelys platynota (Gray, 1834)

71

Family Bataguridae.

Distribution and habitat Malaysia, Sumatra, Java and Borneo, where it may be seen in wet zones of jungle, notably in stagnant water with plenty of swamp vegetation.

Characteristics The very flat carapace measures up to 32 cm (13 in) and is grayish brown or reddish brown with dark radiating lines on each scute; the plastron is orange-yellow with blackish marks on each scute. Food consists of fruit and aquatic plants.

ORIENTAL REGION

137

Malaysian giant turtle

Orlitia borneensis (Gray, 1873)

72

Family Bataguridae.

Distribution and habitat Malaysian peninsula, Borneo (where it is very common) and Sumatra. Strongly aquatic, it frequents the deep waters of large rivers and lakes.

Characteristics The oval carapace is bulky, and larger specimens may grow up to 80 cm (32 in) in length. Because of its aquatic habits, it is seldom observed in the wild and little is known of its way of life. The diet is omnivorous, predominantly made up of small fish caught in the water.

Keeled box turtle
Pyxidea mouhotii (Gray, 1862)

Family Bataguridae.
Distribution and habitat Southern regions of China and the island of Hainan, northern Indochina, Myanmar, Assam and India. It is also found at fair heights and, with its strongly terrestrial habits, will often stray far from water toward woods and forests.

Characteristics The carapace, about 18 cm (7 in), has three prominent keels, flattened dorsally and conspicuously notched at the rear edge. The color is yellowish or reddish brown. The plastron is yellowish, with brownish marks on each scute. It can partially close its shell. Breeding habits are little known. Almost completely herbivorous.

Situation For some years, it has been caught in the wild (above all in Vietnam) for the European collectors' market.

Four-eyed turtle
Sacalia quadriocellata (Siebenrock, 1903)

74

Family
Bataguridae.
Distribution and habitat
Southeast China, the island of Hainan

and Vietnam. It is a resident of rivulets and streams in mountainous zones, especially in woods and jungles. Classification of the genus still in progress has indicated two other species, *S. quadriocellata* (though some regard it as a subspecies of *S. bealei*) and *S. pseudocephala*.

Characteristics The smooth, flattened carapace, nut-brown in color with lighter streaks, measures up to about 15 cm (6 in). The plastron is yellowish with dark markings. There are two bright, black-bordered ocelli on the back of the head (four in *S. quadriocellata*).

The female lays 2 elongated eggs per clutch. The diet is mainly vegetarian.

Black marsh turtle

Siebenrockiella crassicollis (Lindholm, 1929)

Family Bataguridae.

Distribution and habitat Southern Vietnam, Thailand, Malaysia, Sumatra, Java and Borneo. Its ideal habitats are streams, rivers and pools with a muddy bottom and with vegetation on the banks and in the water.

Characteristics The carapace, with three keels, is very dark and up to 20 cm (8 in) long. Its large head has light marks behind each orbit and on jaws. Very timid, it spends long periods half-submerged in the muddy water but may venture onto land to find food and to bask.

The male approaches the female with bobbing movements of the head, neck extended. The female lays 1 to 2 eggs in 3 to 4 clutches a season, hatching in about 80 days. The diet is omnivorous and opportunist; it hunts invertebrates but may feed on aquatic plants and corpses of fish and other small invertebrates.

Vietnam leaf turtle

Annamemys annamensis (Siebenrock, 1903)

Family Bataguridae.

Distribution and habitat It lives in central regions of Vietnam, where it is endemic (to date it has been found only in Phuc-Son and Fai-Fo). Ideal habitats are marshy zones, rice paddies and slow-flowing rivers and streams, especially on flat terrain.

Characteristics The carapace is slightly domed, measuring up to about 18 cm (7 in) long; its color dark gray, brownish gray or blackish. In the young, there are three keels.

The turtle is particularly shy and elusive, and little is known of its life habits apart from its herbivorous diet.

Situation Like other endemic or rare species of Bataguridae, this turtle is caught indiscriminately for eventual export to Western markets, where collectors find it difficult to provide the right conditions for successful breeding. All too often, captured specimens refuse food and die of debilitation.

Indian star tortoise
Geochelone elegans (Schoepff, 1795)

Family Testudinidae.
Distribution and habitat Pakistan, the entire Indian peninsula and Sri Lanka. It may be found in a variety of habitats, both natural and artificial.
Characteristics The very handsome, domed carapace measures up to 28 cm (11 in) long. The female annually produces 2 to 3 clutches of 3 to 10 eggs, which have a very fragile shell. Incubation is lengthy, on average around 120 days.

The diet is mainly herbivorous, but very young individuals, and sometimes adults as well, hunt insects and worms.
Situation In CITES Appendix II and also, since 1972, in List IV of the Indian Wildlife Protection Act. Thanks to such protection and its natural vitality, *G. elegans* is today one of the least endangered of Testudinidae species.

142

River terrapin
Batagur baska (Gray, 1830, in Gray, 1830–1835)

Family Bataguridae.
Distribution and habitat Irrawaddy river basin in Myanmar to southern Thailand and Vietnam, Malaysia and Sumatra. It inhabits estuaries and the banks of medium-size and large rivers.
Characteristics The carapace measures up to 60 cm (2 ft) in length. The adults travel far upstream, to reach the sandbars a banks, where the fema lay their eggs.
Situation Listed in CI Appendix I. Like ot large species of Batag dae, it is under threa capture for its flesh aln everywhere in its ra Equally endangered another very similar s cies, *Callagur borneoe* (Schlegel & Müller, 18 which ranges from T land through Malaysi Sumatra and Borneo, l wise measuring over cm (2 ft) and with a pre lently vegetarian diet. grams of captive breed have been introduced Thailand to repler wild populations.

Yellow-headed tortoise
Indotestudo elongata (Blyth, 1853)

78

143

Family Testudinidae.

Distribution and habitat Myanmar, north-central India, Nepal, Bangladesh, Cambodia, Laos, Malaysia, Thailand, Vietnam and Guangxi region in China. It inhabits evergreen and deciduous forests in hill and mountain areas.

Characteristics It has a massive body, and adults weigh over 3 kg (6½ lb). The carapace, which is yellowish brown or yellowish green with darker markings on the pleural and vertebral scutes, is domed and elongate, measuring up to 32 cm (13 in). During the breeding season, the skin around the eyes and on the snout turns bright pink. The female lays 2 to 4 eggs per clutch. The diet consists of vegetation and fruit, sometimes including fungi.

Situation It is listed in CITES Appendix II. The species is exported from Thailand to Hong Kong to be used in popular Chinese medicines.

Impressed tortoise
Manouria impressa (Günther, 1882)

Family Testudinidae.
Distribution and habitat Yunnan, Guangxi and island of Hainan, in China, Tonkin, in Vietnam, Myanmar, Thailand, Malaysia. It lives in the evergreen forests of mountain zones, from altitudes of 700 m (2,300 ft) to 2,000 m (6,500 ft), often straying some distance from water.

Characteristics The carapace measures 28 cm (11 in). The body is flatter than that of *M. emys,* and the carapace is covered with recessed scutes. Males have a horny caudal hook.

The species is active only in the rainy season, and the female lays 6 to 17 eggs at a time. Food consists primarily of grass and bamboo shoots.

Situation Despite the difficulty of rearing them in captivity (they seldom survive for more than a year), hundreds of specimens are exported every year, mainly from Malaysia, Myanmar (which does not recognize CITES) and Thailand. And many more are killed for their meat and for their plastrons, exported to China as a component in the preparation of traditional medicines. Moreover, destruction of the habitat, even in areas that are theoretically protected (forest tree felling and fires), make this chelonian species one of the most endangered in the world. It is listed in CITES Appendix II.

Travancore tortoise
Indotestudo forstenii (Schlegel & Müller, 1844)

Family Testudinidae.

Distribution and habitat Originating in the states of Karnataka and Kerala in southwest India, this species comprises populations formerly described as *Indotestudo travancorica*. It is an inhabitant of evergreen and partially deciduous tropical forests, up to a height of 1,000 m (3,300 ft).

Characteristics The elongate, domed carapace, with its serrated rear marginal scutes, measures up to 31 cm (12¼ in). The skin around the eyes and nostrils turns pink during the reproductive season. Mating proceeds in three stages: the male moves his head rhythmically to sniff the female, then uses his shell and gular scutes to immobilize her; during copulation, the male emits sharp cries. The female lays 1 to 2 eggs per clutch.

The diet is vegetarian.

Situation Listed in CITES Appendix I as a hunted species. A special reserve has been set up in the Kerala forest.

Asian brown tortoise
Manouria emys (Schlegel & Müller, 1844)

Family Testudinidae.
Distribution and habitat Myanmar, some places in southern China, India (Assam), Sumatra and Bor-neo, Cambodia, Laos, Malaysia, Thailand and Vietnam. There are two recognized subspecies, *M. e. emys* and *M. e. phareyi.*

Some authors maintain that the latter subspecies is synonymous with *M. e. nutapundi.* Others, because of its many differences in biology and natural behavior, define it as a species.

The tortoise lives in monsoon forests and trop-ical woodlands, especially in very moist, shady areas where they often venture into clearings to sunbathe.
Characteristics This is the largest of the Asiatic Tes-tudinidae, with a carapace that in the subspecies *M. e. phareyi* may exceed 60 cm (2 ft) in length. It may be olive, brownish or black. The anterior surface of each foreleg is covered

with large pointed scales. The males, as in other Testudinidae, buffet the females insistently with their carapace and mount them after forcing them to retreat inside their shell. The females lay 5 to 8 eggs, once or twice a year, with up to 50 eggs in all in the subspecies *M. e. phareyi*.

Females of the latter subspecies have been observed using their feet to sweep together a large mass of fallen leaves to create a kind of nest in which to lay their eggs.

The diet is vegetarian, based on leaves, fruit, seeds and also aquatic plants.

Situation Listed in CITES Appendix II, the species is captured for export, mainly from Thailand and Vietnam, to collectors in the United States and Europe. Given their size, it is not uncommon to find specimens, particularly of the subspecies *M. e. emys*, exhibited along with other reptiles.

In their native habitats, they are also hunted for food or sold alive in nearby markets. For all these reasons, they are regarded as locally endangered.

As for other large land tortoises, the principal threat for the populations of Manouria emys *is the continuing reduction and splitting up of their original habitats.*

NEARCTIC SUBREGION

Previous spread, a desert
tortoise, Gopherus berlandieri,
heads for shelter. The North
American tortoises and turtles
are arguably best known
away from their natural
environments and in other
countries abroad. For many
years, turtle farms have been
operating with a view to
breeding and exporting
different species for collections.
Above, mountain woodland on
the Mexican plateau.

NEARCTIC SUBREGION

North America to Gulf of Mexico
and the Mexican high plateau

North America is home to a vast number of chelonian species,
including many pond turtles, which are identified by popular
names that have become scientifically recognized, such as
"cooter," "slider," "terrapin," "box turtle" and "snapping turtle." These species are grouped into three characteristic families: Emydidae (almost exclusively, with the exception of the
European genus *Emys*), Kinosternidae and Chelydridae, with
the two giant forms *Chelydra serpentina* and *Macroclemys temminckii*. The majority of these species are distributed through
the central and eastern regions of the United States, and many
have a range that includes, or is bounded by, the basins of the
Mississippi and the Tennessee Rivers.

Individuals of many of the more common species, such as
Chrysemys picta, *Trachemys scripta*, *Pseudemys concinna*, *P. floridana* and *P. nelsoni*, gather along the banks of rivers and canals
and on quieter shores, where there are handy spots for basking
in the sun. Lagoons and estuaries of brackish water are still the
haunts of *Malaclemys terrapin*, notwithstanding the past mas-

sacres of the species, when the animals were hunted for their meat. More elusive and much more rare, principally due to habitat destruction and widespread water pollution, are *Clemmys muhlenbergii, C. marmorata* and *Pseudemys rubriventris*. Other aquatic turtles, such as *Graptemys barbouri, G. versa, G. caglei, G. oculifera* and *G. flavimaculata,* are also very localized and under threat. The so-called musk turtles and pond turtles, *Kinosternon* and *Sternotherus*, spend much of the day in dense vegetation or well camouflaged in the muddiest parts of ponds and pools.

The three other families represented in the Nearctic subregion are Bataguridae, with *Rhinoclemmys,* the only genus not found in the Old World; Trionychidae, with the genus *Apalone*; and Testudinidae, with the genus *Gopherus*. The latter are associated with arid, subdesert zones and are threatened by extreme temperature, human intervention and excessive hunting for commercial ends. As elsewhere, major conservation programs have been introduced, and suitable areas of protection have been established for particularly endangered species.

Left, a watercourse through Texas swampland. Above, a coastal mangrove swamp. Often the surroundings most suitable for chelonians are those that nowadays are most affected by natural alteration and pollution or which are most subject to human intervention.

Right, a female and male of the Kinosternidae. In this species, there is evident sexual dimorphism in the dimensions of head and body (greater in the males) and in the patterning (bright marks on the sides of the head and on the jaws of the males of certain species). Below, the plastron of Kinosternon (seen from below and from the front). The presence of two movable hinges allows the shell of this genus to close almost completely.

KINOSTERNIDAE

This New World family ranges from Canada to South America, with four genera (*Claudius, Staurotypus, Kinosternon* and *Sternotherus*) and approximately 30 species. Classification of the family has aroused debate: some authors suggest that the genus *Sternotherus* should be abolished and that the species therein attributed to *Kinosternon*; others claim that the genera *Claudius* and *Staurotypus*, which differ in their having maintained entoplastral bones, should properly belong to the family Staurotypidae. Representatives of these families are medium to small in size, the maximum being 38 cm (15 in) in *Staurotypus triporcatus* and the minimum 11 cm (4¼ in) in *Kinosternon depressum*, and possess 10 pairs of peripheral bones on the carapace, with 11 marginal scutes on either side. The plastron may have one or two movable hinges. On the edge of the carapace are two pairs of glands that secrete repellent substances when the turtle senses danger. The species are aquatic but may spend long periods sunbathing on the banks or among the floating vegetation; the majority, however, are active either at dusk or at night. *Sternotherus odoratus* and *S. minor* are capable of clambering a few feet onto tree branches projecting from the water, diving in should danger threaten. Many species inhabit small temporary pools, where they can hide during the months of drought.

Females lay 1 to 9 elliptical eggs with porcelain-like shells, once or twice a year, either in holes or under plants; they hatch within 2 to 3 months. Whereas in the genera *Claudius* and *Staurotypus,* gender of the hatchlings does not depend upon the temperature of egg incubation, that is the norm in *Kinosternon* and *Sternotherus*. Newly born *Kinosternon baurii* are among the tiniest chelonians at birth, measuring barely 16.5 mm (½ in). The diet of the Kinosternidae is highly omnivorous; depending on availability, they feed on various leaves and algae and on small prey such as snails, insects and even dead fish.

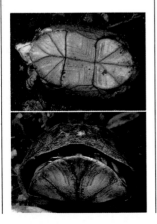

Identifying the genera of present-day Kinosternidae

1. Plastron has at least one movable hinge → 2.
1a. Plastron lacks a movable hinge; bridge joined to carapace by ligaments. Carapace smooth, under 20 cm (8 in) in adults → Claudius.
2. Bridge with large axillary and inguinal scutes; plastron has a single movable hinge; carapace up to 38 cm (15 in) in adults, with three conspic-

uous longitudinal keels → Staurotypus.
2a. Bridge without scutes; 10 to 11 plastral scutes; plastron small; carapace with two movable hinges → 3.
3. In adults, both hinges are movable and functional → Kinosternon.
3a. In adults, only the anterior hinge is functional. Areas of skin present between plastral scutes → Sternotherus.

Plastron of Claudius angustatus *(a); plastron and carapace of* Staurotypus salvinii *(b-c); plastron of* Kinosternon subrubrum *(d); plastron of* Sternotherus carinatus *(e).*

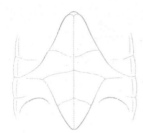

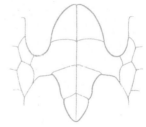

a

b

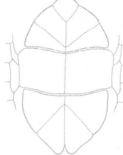

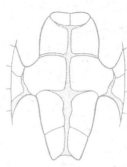

c

d

e

Yellow mud turtle
Kinosternon flavescens (Agassiz, 1857)

Family Kinosternidae.

Distribution and habitat United States and Mexico, with four subspecies: *K. f. flavescens, K. f. arizonense, K. f. spooneri* and *K. f. durangoense*. It lives in almost any slow-moving or still body of water with a muddy bottom and plenty of vegetation.

Characteristics Small, brown, oval, slightly convex carapace, measuring at most 16 cm (6¼ in). Mandible tinted yellow, as are the two pairs of barbels on the chin. On the plastron (left photograph) are 11 scutes with two movable hinges.

The female often lays eggs in rotten tree stumps or in heaps of putrescent plants. The young, in the event of late egg deposition or extreme cold during the months of incubation, may overwinter in the eggs. The diet is omnivorous, with a preference for small aquatic invertebrates.

Situation The subspecies *K. f. spooneri* is threatened by water changes due to pollution and is locally protected.

Rough-footed mud turtle
Kinosternon hirtipes (Wagler, 1830)

Family Kinosternidae.
Distribution and habitat It is found in the Big Bend region of Texas and throughout the Mexican high plateau to Mexico City, with six subspecies: *K. h. hirtipes*, *K. h. murrayi*, *K. h. chapalaense*, *K. h. tarascense*, *K. h. magdalense* and *K. h. megacephalum*. It does not show any special preference as to habitat and may be observed in ponds

and prairie swamps as well as in rivers and lakes.
Characteristics The smooth, oval carapace measures up to 17 cm (7 in). The plastron has 11 scutes and two well-developed hinges.

Habits are almost exclusively aquatic and nocturnal, with brief exits from the water only to move about. The female lays 4 to 7 eggs, 2 to 4 times a year. The diet is carnivorous, based principally on invertebrates such as insect larvae, small snails and annelid worms.
Situation Only the Mexican populations are presently endangered, being caught for food.

Scorpion mud turtle

Kinosternon scorpioides (Linnaeus, 1766)

Distribution and habitat It has a vast range, from the state of Tamaulipas, in Mexico, through Central America to northern Argentina. It is a highly variable species, with several subspecies: *K. s. scorpioides, K. s. carajasensis, K. s. seriei, K. s. albogulare, K. s. cruentatum* and *K. s. abaxillare.* It lives in small and medium-size streams. As a rule, it withstands periods of drought by burying itself in the muddy bottom.

Characteristics The carapace may measure up to 21 cm (8¼ in), and there is a movable hinge on the plastron. The female lays 6 to 12 eggs (according to population, there may be 2 or more clutches annually), with an incubation period of approximately 3 months.

The diet is carnivorous, especially directed toward the hunting of fish.

Common mud turtle
Kinosternon subrubrum (Lacépède, 1788)

Family Kinosternidae.

Distribution and habitat East coast of United States from Connecticut and Long Island to Florida, the Mississippi valley and Texas, with three known subspecies: *K. s. subrubrum* (with a spotted head), *K. s. steindachneri* (with a plain or streaked head) and *K. s. hippocrepis* (with two bright lines on the back of the head).

The turtle lives mainly in fresh water and streams but is also found in more sluggish water with a muddy bottom and plenty of vegetation. It often clambers onto plants for warmth, diving swiftly at the least sign of danger.

Characteristics The carapace measures about 12 cm (5 in) long and ranges from olive to dark brown, without patterns or bulges. The plastron has two well-developed movable hinges.

The species is active from mid-March to October. In months of drought, it migrates toward permanent pools or buries itself in the muddy bottom for the summer.

Males are quite aggressive and may defend their own small territory. Mating usually takes place in shallow water and at night, so little is known about their behavior during this phase.

Females (especially of the southerly populations) lay several clutches of 1 to 6 elliptical eggs a year. These are often deposited in tunnels dug by muskrats or in the nests of alligators. There is a long period of incubation, generally lasting about 100 days.

The diet is omnivorous, consisting mainly of prey caught by patrolling the bottom but also, importantly, of aquatic plants.

Situation It is much sought after for collections.

Mexican mud turtle
Kinosternon integrum (LeConte, 1854)

Family Kinosternidae.
Distribution and habitat Central and eastern Mexico, from southern Chihuahua to Oaxaca. It lives in streams and rivers with large, deep pools.
Characteristics The oval carapace measures up to 20 cm (8 in), its color varying greatly from brownish yellow to gray. The plastron is double-hinged. The head is big, with a long snout and hooked jaws. On the neck are two large barbels and other smaller ones. The diet is predominantly carnivorous.

Striped mud turtle
Kinosternon baurii (Garman, 1891)

Family Kinosternidae.
Distribution and habitat From southern Georgia to the Florida peninsula. It lives in ponds, swamps and drainage channels.
Characteristics The carapace measures up to 12 cm (5 in) in length. There are 11 scutes with two large hinges on the plastron. Three long, shiny stripes adorn the smooth, even carapace (older specimens have dark stripes). Behavior is markedly terrestrial. There are 3 or more clutches a year, from September to June, each comprising 1 to 4 eggs, which hatch after incubating for some 130 days. The diet is omnivorous, including invertebrates, vegetation and dead fish.
Situation Locally, at least, it is endangered by modifications to its confined wet habitats.

Family Kinosternidae.
Distribution and habitat
United States, from southern Mississippi to Texas. It inhabits sluggish rivers, streams with a soft bottom and abundant vegetation, and ponds.

Characteristics The carapace, with a very pronounced medial keel, measures up to 15 cm (6 in) long. The yellow plastron has 10 scutes, with one inconspicuous hinge. Barbels are present only on the chin. Local populations are fairly numerous, with up to 100 individuals an acre. The species is active from March to November.

Mating occurs underwater at night. There are 2 clutches of 4 to 7 eggs a season, with an incubation period of 100 to 120 days. It is omnivorous, hunting insects, crustaceans and tadpoles.

Situation It is caught and killed at times as a result of fishing with nets and traps.

Common musk turtle
Sternotherus odoratus (Latreille, 1801)

Family Kinosternidae.
Distribution and habitat Canada and United States, from southern Ontario and Maine to Florida, Texas and Wisconsin. It lives in sluggish or flowing water with a muddy bottom.
Characteristics The smooth, high-domed carapace is up

to 13.7 cm (5½ in) long. There are two bright stripes on the head, with barbels on the chin and throat. The species is aquatic by habit but basks for long periods ashore. Mating takes place underwater, with nests dug between February and June. Each clutch contains 1 to 9 elliptical eggs, which hatch in 60 to 80 days. It is popularly known as the "stinkpot," for it ejects a foul-smelling, yellowish secretion from two pairs of musk glands located under the edge of the carapace, sufficient to scare off small carnivores. The males are aggressive and bite if disturbed.

Loggerhead musk turtle

Sternotherus minor (Agassiz, 1857)

Family Kinosternidae.
Distribution and habitat United States, in Georgia, Florida, Mississippi, Louisiana and Tennessee, with two subspecies, *S. m. minor* and *S. m. peltifer*. It is found in streams, rivers, swamps and ponds.
Characteristics Carapace up to 13.5 cm (5½ in). Indistinct hinge between the scutes of the plastron. Barbels present on the chin. Up to 4 clutches of 2 to 3 eggs hatch in 70 to 100 days.

The young hunt insects, the adults chiefly mollusks. It emits a musky smell.

Flattened musk turtle

Sternotherus depressus
(Tinkle & Webb, 1955)

Family Kinosternidae.
Distribution and habitat United States, but exclusively in the basin of the Black Warrior River, Alabama. The water in which it lives must have a rocky bottom. It may interbreed with *S. minor* in areas shared by both species.
Characteristics The much flattened carapace measures up to 11 cm (4¼ in) long. The head and neck are greenish, with conspicuous black lines. Barbels are found only on the neck. The diet is carnivorous.

Little is known of its behavior in the wild because of its particularly elusive habits of mating in the water at night and laying eggs in lairs of mammals on shore.
Situation The species is at risk because of its restricted area of distribution.

CHELYDRIDAE

This is a family with only two living genera and a range limited to the Americas. The snapping turtles, so called because of the manner in which they hunt, are among the biggest of all freshwater turtles. They retain a body structure with several primitive characteristics: a huge head with powerful hooked jaws, a long tail covered with thick, partially overlapping scales, a relatively small plastron in the shape of a cross, and a carapace with 12 marginal scutes on either side. The males are larger than the females, which lay numerous eggs in a single annual clutch. The diet is carnivorous and opportunist, often including carrion. This semiaquatic species is found in wet zones of every sort.

In many countries, their import is prohibited because, should they escape from breeding farms into their natural environment, they are considered dangerous to humans.

Identifying the genera of present-day Chelydridae

1. Upper jaw hooked; carapace with three long, very prominent keels running the whole length of the back (b, d) → Macroclemys.

2. Upper jaw barely hooked; the carapace keels do not run the length of the back (a, c) → Chelydra.

Side view of the skull of Chelydra *(c) and of* Macroclemys *(d). It is noticeable (see also the drawings at left) that the upper jaw of* Macroclemys *(b) is much more sharply hooked than that of* Chelydra *(b).*

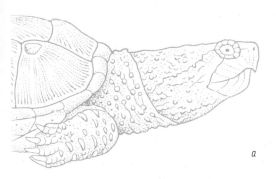

a

c

b

d

Snapping turtle
Chelydra serpentina (Linnaeus, 1758)

Family Chelydridae. **Distribution and habitat** Southern Canada to Ecuador, with four subspecies: *C. s. serpentina, C. s. osceola, C. s. rossignonii* and *C. s. acutirostris.*

The populations of Central and South America may be ascribed to a different species, given also the separation of the range from that of North America. The turtle lives in all types of water, burying itself in the muddy bed or remaining hidden among the aquatic vegetation.

Characteristics The carapace measures up to 47 cm (19 in) and weighs up to 21 kg (46 lb), the record being 60 cm (2 ft) and 37.4 kg (82 lb). The description "snapping turtle" derives from the powerful bite of the jaws in the huge head. The carapace is light brown with variations to dark brown, and it is often covered with algae or mud. There are tubercles on the neck. Copulation takes place between April and November, with 25 to 83 eggs laid mainly in June.

These hatch in 60 to 125 days, depending on the weather. In temperate areas, the young overwinter in the nest. Females are capable of storing spermatozoa for several years and often travel considerable distances from the mating site to lay their eggs. It is an omnivorous species, eating invertebrates, aquatic plants, crustaceans, fish, birds and small mammals. **Situation** It is regarded as a dangerous species, and therefore, importation for breeding is prohibited in many countries. In North America, it is hunted for its flesh and actively traded in many places.

Alligator snapping turtle
Macroclemys temminckii (Troost, 1836)

Family Chelydridae.

Distribution and habitat United States, from Georgia to Florida, Texas, Iowa and southern Illinois and Indiana. It lives in deep rivers and lakes and occasionally in ponds and brackish water.

Characteristics This is one of the biggest freshwater turtles in the world, holding the record for maximum weight of 99.5 kg (220 lb). The carapace, which ranges from gray to brown, varies in length from 34 cm (14 in) to more than 66 cm (26 in). The head is massive, with strongly hooked jaws, and the tail is very long. The pink, wormlike structure of the tongue serves as a movable lure to attract prey, from fish to small mammals. Mating takes place in the water between February and April, and there is 1 clutch annually, from April to June, of 10 to 52 round eggs that hatch in 80 to 112 days. Only the females leave the water to lay the eggs.

Situation The meat is in demand for turtle soup, so the species is becoming quite rare in much of its range.

Painted wood turtle

Rhinoclemmys pulcherrima (Gray, 1855)

Family Bataguridae.

Distribution and habitat It belongs to the single genus of Bataguridae in the Nearctic subregion, distributed from the west coast of Mexico (Sonora state) to Costa Rica, with four subspecies: *R. p. pulcherrima*, *R. p. rogerbarbouri*, *R. p. incisa* and *R. p. manni*; the last, because of its variegated design, is one of the most beautiful of all turtles. The species is terrestrial, living deep in the undergrowth of wet woods (the photograph shows a typical habitat in Mexico); it seeks water during droughts and is active after heavy downpours.

Characteristics

The carapace measures up to 20 cm (8 in) and varies in color according to subspecies, from plain brown to a mottled pattern of streaks and ocelli, red or yellow edged with black. The head and neck are very colorful, with alternating reddish or orange stripes. The female lays 1 to 5 eggs 2 or 3 times a year. Omnivorous, mainly vegetation.

THE SUBSPECIES OF
RHINOCLEMMYS PULCHERRIMA

Rhinoclemmys pulcherrima rogerbarbouri, from Sonora to Colima (Mexico); very wide, rather flat carapace, more or less uniformly brown.

Rhinoclemmys pulcherrima pulcherrima, in Guerrero (Mexico); wide, flat carapace, basically brown, with circular, dark-bordered red or yellow spots on each pleural scute.

Rhinoclemmys pulcherrima incisa, from Oaxaca (Mexico) to northern parts of Nicaragua; more or less domed carapace, with a line or large, black-bordered red or yellow ocellus on each pleural scute and a pale band on each marginal scute.

Rhinoclemmys pulcherrima manni, from southern Nicaragua to northern Costa Rica; carapace highly domed, brownish, with red or yellow ocelli on each pleural scute and two pale bands on each marginal scute.

Top left, an adult male of Rhinoclemmys pulcherrima pulcherrima. *Top right, frontal view of* Rhinoclemmys pulcherrima incisa *and, above, ventral view of plastrons of two individuals of the same subspecies. Left, an adult of* Rhinoclemmys pulcherrima manni.

EMYDIDAE

This is one of the largest living families of turtles, found principally in the United States. With the exception of members of the genus *Terrapene*—commonly known as "box turtles," thanks to the pronounced mobility of the anterior and posterior lobes of the plastron—the carapace of the Emydidae species is rather flat, oval and smooth-surfaced. This characteristic structure is the result of the strongly aquatic habits of the group, few of which are found far from water. Powerful swimmers, very swift and agile in their movements, these turtles are active in their search for food, and the species are adept hunters of slippery prey such as small fish. Yet their diet is greatly varied: as a rule, they are omnivores, and some species, which in the juvenile phase are carnivores, may gradually modify their habits and become vegetarian as adults.

The turtles seek out dry, well-exposed spots for warmth, and dozens of individuals will sometimes compete to stake out a place in the sun.

Courtship proceeds in a series of elaborate phases, almost invariably underwater. Males of *Chrysemys*, *Pseudemys* and *Trachemys* position themselves before the females and rub against the head and neck of their partners with frenzied movements of their long-clawed forefeet. The number of clutches and eggs varies according to the species, the dimensions of the female and the latitude. On average, the female lays 5 to 25 elliptical eggs in a small hole dug for the purpose. Species that live in the more northerly regions deposit eggs only once a year, whereas those farther south, benefiting from warm temperatures, will do so two or three times.

The family contains a number of species with a wide distribution and high popularity as pets. For more than 30 years, breeding farms in the southern United States have raised these elegant species, known for their sturdiness and vitality, virtually on an industrial scale.

Over the years, millions of very young specimens have been exported and sold all over the world, and in some cases, notably where pets have been abandoned and the climate is favorable, individuals have become naturalized anew and caused damage to local wildlife (Saudi Arabia, South Africa and France).

Above, Emys orbicularis. *Except for the single genus* Emys *(of which this is the sole species), the family of Emydidae is found almost exclusively in North America. Below, two young specimens of* Pseudemys floridana. *This is the most common species reared in home surroundings. Bottom,* Trachemys scripta elegans, *surely the most widespread species in the world today, thanks to thoughtless release into the wild by thousands of indifferent pet owners.*

Identifying the genera of present-day Emydidae

1. *Plastron, at least in young adults, with a functional hinge between pectoral and abdominal scutes* → **2.**
1a. *Plastron always without a hinge* → **4.**
2. *Anterior and posterior lobes of plastron completely close (except in very young specimens) apertures of shell. Carapace markedly domed* → Terrapene.
2a. *Lobes of plastron only partially close apertures of shell* → **3.**
3. *Elongated head and neck, measuring about half the length of carapace; chin and throat bright yellow* → Emydoidea.
3a. *Average head and neck, measuring about half the length of carapace. Single Old World genus of Emydidae* → Emys.
4. *Crest or series of extended tubercles on inner surface of upper jaw, parallel to its edge* → 5.
4a. *Smooth, barely undulating inner surface of upper jaw* → **6.**
5. *Carapace smooth, without keels, and rear edge not serrated* → Chrysemys.
5a. *Carapace with longitudinal ridges or with a keel of varying extent, but not both; the rear edge of carapace may be serrated* → Pseudemys.
6. *Inner surface of upper jaw thin, the innermost ridge parallel to the cutting edge* → 7.
6a. *Inner surface of upper jaw without a tuberculate ridge parallel to the cutting edge* → Trachemys.
7. *Head and neck together as long as carapace* → Deirochelys.
7a. *Head and neck together at most half the length of carapace* → **8.**
8. *Cutting edge of upper jaw thin* → Clemmys.
8a. *Cutting edge of upper jaw very broad* → **9.**
9. *Scutes of carapace with concentric ridges and areolae; pale-colored head and neck, speckled or blotched, without longitudinal streaks* → Malaclemys.
9a. *Scutes of carapace smooth, without concentric ridges; head and neck with conspicuous longitudinal streaks* → Graptemys.

Ventral view of skulls of Clemmys (a), with the cutting surface of the narrow upper jaw, and of Malaclemys (b), with its much broader cutting surface.

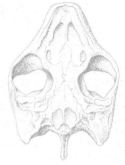

a

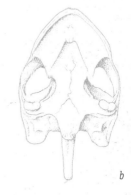

b

Painted tortoise
Chrysemis picta (Schneider, 1783)

Family
Emydidae.
Distribution and habitat
From southern Canada to Georgia, Louisiana and scattered regions in the Southwest, and in Chihuahua, Mexico, with four subspecies which may interbreed: *C. p. picta*, *C. p. marginata*, *C. p. dorsalis* and *C. p. bellii*. It inhabits tranquil streams, rivers and lakes.
Characteristics The carapace, olive to black, is oval, smooth and flat, up to 25 cm (10 in) long. The scutes may be edged with green, yellow or red. Eggs are laid between May and July, with 1 to 2 clutches among northern populations, 2 to 4 farther south. Each clutch of 2 to 20 elliptical eggs hatches in 65 to 80 days. In cold climates, the young overwinter in the nest. Males reach sexual maturity in 2 to 5 years, females in 4 to 8. The young are carnivores, the adults vegetarians.

THE SUBSPECIES OF *CHRYSEMIS PICTA*

Chrysemis picta picta, from southeastern Canada and along the eastern coastline of the United States to northern Georgia and eastern Alabama; the plastron is yellow, without marks (top photograph).

Chrysemis picta marginata, from southern Quebec to Ontario and in the southern United States in Tennessee and Alabama; the plastron is yellow, with a dark central patch.

Chrysemis picta dorsalis, from southern Illinois to the Gulf of Mexico and from Oklahoma to Alabama; the carapace has a reddish or yellow vertebral stripe, and the plastron is yellow, without marks (photograph on facing page, top).

Chrysemis picta bellii, from western Ontario to Missouri, Oregon and British Columbia; clear lines on the carapace (photograph below, a young specimen; right, bottom, an adult); the yellow plastron has an intricate dark pattern (photograph on facing page, bottom).

Distribution of Chrysemys picta.

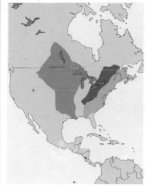

■	C. p. picta
■	C. p. marginata
■	C. p. dorsalis
■	C. p. bellii

Spotted turtle
Clemmys guttata (Schneider, 1792)

Family Emydidae.

Distribution and habitat The range of this species extends from southern Canada and along the entire eastern coastline of the United States to northern Florida. Preferred habitats include swamps and wet woodland and pools, rivers and streams with a muddy bed and abundant vegetation. It may spend much time ashore in the underbrush.

Characteristics It is a small turtle, with a carapace measuring at most 12.5 cm (5 in) in length. The smooth black carapace is handsomely patterned with an abundance of yellow spots. Spots of the same color adorn the head, neck and legs. Males have brown eyes; and females, orange.

The average body temperature for activity is considerably lower than that required by other turtles. Reproduction occurs

in spring and is always preceded by an elaborate courtship on the part of the males.

Females dig their nests (usually in June) in sunny places. Each clutch comprises 3 to 8 elliptical eggs with flexible shells. The young hatch at the end of August to September or may overwinter in the nest. Adults, however, spend the winter in soft mud, in heaps of vegetation or in the abandoned tunnels of muskrats. The species is omnivorous, with a high percentage of insect prey; it also feeds on aquatic plants, algae and small amphibians.

Wood turtle
Clemmys insculpta (LeConte, 1830)

95

173

Family Emydidae.
Distribution and habitat In Canada, in Nova Scotia, Quebec and Ontario (Great Lakes region) and in the United States, in New York, Virginia, Ohio, Michigan, Wisconsin, Minnesota and Iowa. It is one of the most markedly terrestrial of the North American Emydidae species, frequenting a variety of habitats, from streams in deciduous woodland to swamps and marshes.
Characteristics The carapace, measuring up to 23 cm (9 in) long, is formed of flat, rough, pyramidal scutes with irregular edges. The skin of the neck and legs is often reddish orange. The phase preceding copulation, which subsequently takes place in water, has been likened to a protracted dance of the two partners. The female lays 7 to 8 elliptical eggs with flexible shells, which incubate for around 80 days. Hatchlings are born in September and October.

Studies have shown that it is unusually intelligent (with a marked ability for learning and adaptation); it is also very agile, using its strong claws for climbing and clinging to obstacles up to 180 cm (6 ft) in height. The diet is omnivorous and opportunist: in fields flooded after heavy rain, it may catch and devour earthworms and other invertebrates.
Situation Numbers are falling fast as a result of hunting and the disappearance of its natural habitats. Consequently, it appears in CITES Appendix II and is protected as an endangered or threatened species in various North American states.

Chicken turtle
Deirochelys reticularia (Latreille, 1802)

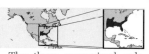

The three recognized sub-species are *D. r. reticularia*, *D. r. chrysea* and *D. r. miaria*. It is found in shallow pools and ponds with plenty of vegetation and in sluggish and near-stagnant streams.

Characteristics The carapace measures up to 25 cm (10 in) long. There are 3 to 5 clutches annually, each comprising 5 to 15 eggs, which hatch in 70 to 100 days. The diet is omnivorous.

Situation Until a few years ago, it was caught and sold for its meat in the southern states, which gave rise to its popular name of "chicken turtle."

Family Emydidae.

Distribution and habitat Along the southeastern coastlines of the United States, from Virginia to Florida, and west to Mississippi, Alabama, Missouri, Arkansas, Oklahoma and Texas.

174

Pacific pond turtle
Clemmys marmorata (Baird & Girard, 1852)

Family Emydidae.

Distribution and habitat In the western United States, from the Cascade Range to the Sierra Nevadas, from southernmost British Columbia to Baja California. The two subspecies are *C. m. marmorata* and *C. m. pallida*. It inhabits ponds and small lakes with abundant vegetation but also irrigated fields and slow-flowing streams.

Characteristics The smooth carapace, olive-green to dark brown with lines and spots, measures up to 19 cm (8 in). Markedly aquatic, the turtle ventures ashore only to bask and lay eggs. The single annual clutch, from April to August, of 3 to 11 eggs hatches in about 70 days. It is an omnivore, with a preference for worms, insects, fish and crustaceans.

Situation Threatened by the drainage of wet zones.

Blanding's turtle

Emydoidea blandingii (Holbrook, 1838)

97

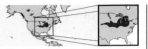

Family Emydidae.

Distribution and habitat North America, from central southern Canada to eastern United States (New Hampshire, Massachusetts and New York), with a very fragmented distribution. It is found in watery habitats of all kinds, typically swamps and bogs, and preferably where the bottom is soft, with abundant vegetation.

Characteristics The smooth, helmet-shaped carapace measures up to 27 cm (11 in) long. Females lay several annual clutches of 5 to 8 eggs, which hatch after 60 to 80 days. The diet is omnivorous.

Situation It is threatened by the disappearance of suitable habitats and by its appeal to the collectors' market.

175

NEARCTIC SUBREGION

Muhlenberg's turtle

Clemmys muhlenbergii (Schoepff, 1801)

Family Emydidae.

Distribution and habitat Along the east coast of the United States, in New York, Massachusetts and Connecticut, but also locally in New Jersey, Pennsylvania, Delaware and Maryland. It prefers shallow, slow-flowing water—sunny ponds and bogs, springtime pools and flooded pastureland.

Characteristics The carapace, up to 11.5 cm (4½ in), is brown to light brown, and the plastron is darker with a yellow central part. Two large yellow, orange or reddish spots are visible on the sides of the head.

The species is active from April to mid-October. Mating takes place in spring, with a single clutch of 3 to 6 elliptical eggs, which hatch in August or September after 40 to 60 days. The diet is omnivorous.

Texas map turtle
Graptcmys versa (Stejniger, 1925)

Family Emydidae.
Distribution and habitat It lives exclusively in the central part of Texas in small tributaries of the Colorado River, especially in stretches with twists and bends and a moderate current.
Characteristics The cara-

pace is elliptical and nearly flat, serrated at the back, and olive-green with yellow lines. Females are larger than the males; in the former, the carapace measures up to 19 cm (8 in), in the latter up to 12 cm (5 in).

During courtship, the male performs character-istic darting movements of the head. The diet is opportunist, but very little is known of the biology of this species.
Situation Like other species of *Graptemys*, the turtle is under threat from water pollution and cap-ture for collections.

Barbour's map turtle
Graptemys barbouri (Carr & Marchand, 1942)

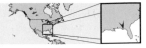

Family Emydidae.
Distribution and habitat Basin of Apalachicola River in Florida and Georgia. It favors flowing water with a rocky or stony bed.
Characteristics The carapace of the male measures up to 13 cm (5 in), and that of the female up to 32 cm (12 in).

Males court the females by facing them and trying to touch them with their head and feet. They lay 6 to 9 eggs in May and June that hatch in 80 to 100 days. The diet is carnivorous, with prey varying in size according to gender.

Ringed map turtle
Graptemys oculifera (Baur, 1890)

Family Emydidae.
Distribution and habitat It occurs only in the basin of the Pearl River of Mississippi and Louisiana, living in small tributaries with plenty of concealment and a strong current.
Characteristics Females may measure up to 22 cm (9 in) in length, males only 11 cm (4¼ in). The marginal scutes have black-bordered yellow or orange ocelli. One or two annual clutches each comprise 3 to 6 eggs, hatching in about 90 days. The diet is mainly carnivorous, basically aquatic mollusks.

Black-knobbed sawback turtle

Graptemys nigrinoda (Cagle, 1954)

Family Emydidae.
Distribution and habitat Widely found in the states of Alabama and Mississippi, in the basins of the Alabama, Tombigbee and

Black Warrior Rivers. The two known subspecies are *G. n. nigrinoda* and *G. n. delticola*. It lives in rivers with a moderate current, sandy bottom and suffi-

cient floating vegetation on which to bask for long periods in the sun.
Characteristics The carapace of the males is up to 10 cm (4 in) long; that of the females up to 15 cm (6 in). The back of the carapace is conspicuous for the blackish knobs on each vertebral scute.

Mating takes place after a protracted courtship by the male, who uses the long claws of his forefeet to stroke the female's snout. Each clutch contains 3 to 6 eggs.

The diet is carnivorous, predominantly comprising small invertebrates.

False map turtle
Graptemys pseudogeographica (Gray, 1831)

102

179

Family Emydidae.
Distribution and habitat The species occurs in the United States, along the Mississippi River and its various tributaries, from the state of Wisconsin to Louisiana. It frequents many types of watery habitats, provided there is plenty of vegetation and suitable dry land for bask-

ing in the sun.
Characteristics The carapace measures up to 27 cm (11 in). Females lay several clutches a year, each with about a dozen eggs that hatch in 60 to 70 days. As in other *Graptemys* species, temperature plays a part in determining gender—producing prevalently male hatchlings when the incubation temperature is below 25°C (77°F) and females at higher temperatures up to 35°C (95°F).

The diet is omnivorous, basically comprising small aquatic animals and plants.

Mississippi map turtle
Graptemys kohni (Baur, 1890)

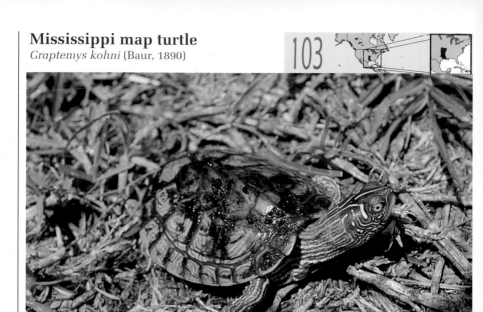

Family Emydidae.
Distribution and habitat
Widely diffused over central southern United States: Mississippi valley, from Illinois and Nebraska to Louisiana, Mississippi and Alabama. Recent studies (Vogt, 1980) consider this form to be a subspecies of *G. pseudogeographica*. It inhabits rivers and lakes

in sheltered zones with an abundance of vegetation.
Characteristics The carapace, olive-green or brownish, measures up to 25 cm (10 in). Blackish keel with tubercles on the posterior vertebral scutes. A crescent-shaped yellow stripe runs laterally beneath the eyes, which have a white iris. Two clutches of 2 to 10 eggs are laid in June. The diet is omnivorous, mainly aquatic plants.
Situation Along with *Trachemys scripta*, this is one of the most popular turtles sold and kept as pets. Very timid and delicate, however, it does not often survive long in captivity.

Cooter
Pseudemys floridana (LeConte, 1830)

Family Emydidae.

Distribution and habitat United States, in the eastern coastal regions of Virginia to Texas, in the Mississippi basin to Illinois and Oklahoma. There are three recognized subspecies: *P. f. floridana*, *P. f. peninsularis* and *P. f. hoyi*. It adapts well to any type of aquatic environment with abundant aquatic vegetation and basking sites.

Characteristics The carapace, up to 40 cm (16 in), exhibits a broad white stripe on the second pleural scute. The plastron is yellowish. A gregarious species, groups of 20 to 30 individuals may be observed basking together. Males perform an insistent dance underwater that culminates only in mating. Females build 2 or more clutches annually, each with 8 to 29 eggs. The more carnivorous diet of the young becomes more herbivorous in adults, based on various aquatic plants.

Florida red-bellied cooter
Pseudemys nelsoni (Carr, 1938)

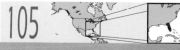

Family Emydidae.
Distribution and habitat
The species is found in the Okefenokee swamps of southern Georgia and westward through the Apalachicola area of Florida. In places of contact, it may interbreed with *P. concinna* and *P. floridana*. It flourishes in all types of aquatic environments, including near-stagnant water with plenty of vegetation.
Characteristics The long, domed carapace may measure up to 34 cm (14 in) and is blackish, with red or yellow spots on the pleural and marginal scutes. In adults, the plastron is reddish orange. It likes to bask on semisubmerged logs or floating aquatic plants. Mating takes place after a courtship stage similar to that described for *Trachemys scripta elegans*. Females may lay up to 6 clutches a year, each of 12 eggs. Whereas the young are to some extent carnivorous, the adults prefer a vegetarian diet.

Family Emydidae.
Distribution and habitat United States, from central New Jersey to North Carolina, with an isolated population in Massachusetts. There are two subspecies: *P. r. rubriventris* and *P. r. bangsi*.

It prefers large bodies of water, such as canals, lakes and ponds, with basking sites.
Characteristics The carapace, measuring up to 40 cm (16 in) in length, is very dark, with reddish and yellowish spots on the marginal and pleural scutes. The plastron is reddish. Like other species of the genus, mating occurs after the male

has courted the female with a vigorous aquatic dance display, waving the long claws of the forefeet close to her snout. The female lays several clutches during the year, each comprising 10 to 17 eggs that hatch in about

100 days. The diet is omnivorous, with a high proportion of aquatic plants.
Situation The subspecies *P. r. bangsi* is found only in small ponds of water in Plymouth County, Massachusetts, with a population estimated to comprise at most 200 individuals; consequently, it is officially regarded as endangered. Since 1984, the federal program has provided for the recovery of very young wild specimens, keeping them under controlled conditions for several months until they have reached a suitable size to be released into an area that offers more security than their original range.

River cooter
Pseudemys concinna (LeConte, 1830)

Family Emydidae.
Distribution and habitat United States, from the eastern seaboard of Virginia and the Carolinas to northern Florida, Georgia and westward to Texas and New Mexico. There are two known subspecies: *P. c. concinna* and *P. c. hieroglyphica*. It lives principally in rivers with a rocky bed and abundant aquatic vegetation, but it may also inhabit other types of aquatic habitats.
Characteristics The carapace measures up to 32 cm (13 in) long and bears an elaborate design that includes a conspicuous white C-shaped mark on

the second pleural scute. The plastron has dark patterns.

Prior to mating underwater, the male courts the female, stroking her head with his long-clawed forefeet. The female lays several clutches during the year, each composed of 6 to 19 eggs. The diet is predominantly herbivo-

rous, with an emphasis on aquatic plants such as *Lemna* and *Ceratophyllum* and threadlike algae. It also hunts and eats small animals.
Situation After *Chrysemys picta*, it is one of the most common and widespread U.S. species and is likewise reared industrially to supply the international collectors' trade. The species, in fact, often appears in pet shops, usually mingled with specimens of *Trachemys scripta elegans* and *T. s. scripta*, although it is not as hardy or adaptable as these.

Family
Emydidae.
Distribution and habitat
In the eastern and southern states along the coast from Cape Cod to the lagoons of southern Texas.

Seven subspecies: *M. t. terrapin*, *M. t. centrata*, *M. t. tequesta*, *M. t. rhizophorarum*, *M. t. macrospilota*, *M. t. pileata* and *M. t. littoralis*.

The terrapin is found in estuaries, lagoons and coastal swamps where the water is variably brackish.
Characteristics The carapace, up to 23 cm (9 in), varies from grayish to brown and black, with dorsal scutes that appear sculpted as a result of growth furrows. The head has bulging eyes and pale jaws.

Females nest twice a year, laying 4 to 18 eggs. Incubation lasts for about 90 days.

The diet is mainly carnivorous, based on small aquatic animals, but with the casual addition of parts of water plants.
Situation For a century or so, the species was hunted indiscriminately for its meat, which was considered a delicacy; this and the systematic destruction of much of its habitat resulted in its becoming rare throughout its range. Today, thanks to protection and changes in outdated eating habits, the species is gradually recovering its numbers and may be regarded as no longer under threat.

Coahuilan box turtle

Terrapene coahuila (Schmidt & Owens, 1944)

Family Emydidae.

Distribution and habitat It lives exclusively in the mountain zone of the basin of the Cuatro Cienegas River in Coahuila, Mexico, found in wet places with plenty of aquatic vegetation.

Characteristics The carapace, which measures up to 16.8 cm (6½ in) long, is slightly domed and greenish or uniformly brown, and the vertebral section is flattened.

It is the only completely aquatic species of the genus *Terrapene* and will immediately dive to the bottom, remaining there for a long time, if it senses danger.

Mating will take place either in water or on land, after a vigorous courtship by the male, who repeatedly bumps the female with his carapace. There are several clutches a year, each with 1 to 4 eggs.

Omnivorous, it hunts small prey in the water or ashore, supplementing this with aquatic plants.

Situation Listed in CITES Appendix I. In spite of the high density of the populations in the wettest parts of its environment (reportedly 133 to 156 adults per hectare), the species is threatened by its extremely localized habitat. A breeding center has been set up in Mexico City.

Ornate box turtle
Terrapene ornata (Agassiz, 1857)

Family Emydidae.
Distribution and habitat Central and southern United States, from Illinois, Iowa and South Dakota to Louisiana, Texas and north-

ern Mexico. The two known subspecies are *T. o. ornata* and *T. o. luteola*. It lives on the sandy soil of prairies and meadows, near suitable rivers, streams and ponds.

Characteristics The carapace, rounded and highly domed, is up to 14 cm (6 in)—longer in females. The iris of the male is reddish; that of the female, brownish yellow. The hinge of the plastron becomes functional from the age of four years. The species remains active from March to October. Copulation is preceded by an assiduous courtship by the males. One or two clutches of 4 to 6 eggs are laid in May and June, with an incubation period of about 70 days. The diet is prevalently carnivorous, consisting of insects such as grasshoppers and beetles.

Eastern box turtle
Terrapene carolina (Linnaeus, 1758)

111

Family
Emydidae.
Distribution and habitat
Central and southern United States and Mexico to Yucatán Peninsula. There are four subspecies found in the United States (*T. c. carolina, T. c. major, T. c. triunguis* and *T. c. bauri*) and two subspecies in Mexico (*T. c. yucatana* and *T. c. mexicana*).

The turtle lives in woodland and forest clearings, in underbrush and sparse vegetation and on shrubby prairies.

Characteristics The length of the carapace is at most 20 cm (8 in), highly domed and variable in color, depending on the subspecies concerned.

Mating is preceded by an elaborate courtship phase, during which the male circles, bites, shoves and attempts to mount the female. The female may store the spermatozoa in a seminal receptacle situated in the oviduct and lay eggs as much as four years after copulation. The species lays several clutches in the course of a year, normally laying 4 to 5 eggs that hatch in 70 to 90 days.

The diet is omnivorous, with an emphasis on small invertebrates.

THE SUBSPECIES OF
TERRAPENE CAROLINA

Terrapene carolina carolina (Linnaeus, 1758), in Maine, Georgia, Michigan, Illinois and Tennessee. Color of shell extremely variable. The subspecies has four toes on each hind foot. Strictly terrestrial, it enters water only very occasionally. The female lays 4 to 6 flexible-shelled eggs per clutch.

Terrapene carolina major (Agassiz, 1857), along the Gulf Coast of United States from Florida to Texas. This is the largest subspecies, with the carapace often measuring more than 20 cm (8 in); the rear margin is flared like a fan. The hind feet have four toes.

Terrapene carolina triunguis (Agassiz, 1857), from Missouri to Alabama and Texas. Carapace is pale olive-green. As the name indicates, the hind feet have only three toes.

Above, top to bottom:
Terrapene carolina carolina,
T. c. bauri *and* T. c. yucatana.
Top left, T. c. carolina; *left,*
T. c. bauri.

Distribution range of Terrapene carolina.

 T. c. carolina

 T. c. major

 T. c. triunguis

 T. c. bauri

T. c. yucatana

 T. c. mexicana

Below, Terrapene carolina major
Top right, T. c. triunguis
Right, T. c. yucatana

Terrapene carolina bauri (Taylor, 1895), on the Florida peninsula and the Keys. The carapace is quite variegated, often with radial lines. The hind feet have only three toes.

Terrapene carolina yucatana (Boulenger, 1895), in Mexico, on the Yucatán Peninsula and in the states of Yucatán, Quintana Roo and Campeche. Elongate, highly domed carapace; the posterior marginals slightly fan-shaped. The hind feet have four toes.

Terrapene carolina mexicana (Gray, 1849), in Mexican states of Tamaulipas, San Luis Potosí and Veracruz. Carapace highly domed, uniformly pale yellow with dark spots. The hind feet have only three toes.

112

Pond slider

Trachemys scripta (Schoepff, 1792)

Family Emydidae.

Distribution and · habitat Almost the entire United States, Mexico, Central America and South America as far as northern Brazil. There are many differentiated subspecies: *T. s. scripta*, *T. s. elegans*, *T. s. troostii*, *T. s. taylori*, *T. s. cataspila*, *T. s. venusta*, *T. s. yaquia*, *T. s. hiltoni*, *T. s. nebulosa*, *T. s. ornata*, *T. s. grayi*, *T. s. callirostris* and *T. s. chichiriviche*.

These turtles frequent all types of freshwater habitats where there is abundant vegetation and suitable opportunity for basking.

Characteristics Maximum carapace dimensions vary according to the sub-species: measurements range from a minimum of 21 cm (8¼ in) in *T. s. troostii* to a maximum of 60 cm (2 ft) in *T. s, grayi*.

Only the males of certain subspecies exhibit long claws on the forefeet. These males perform a courtship ritual, swimming in front of the females, excitedly vibrating and stroking her head with the claws. Males of subspecies that lack those claws persuade the females to mate by sharply nipping their limbs.

THE SUBSPECIES OF *TRACHEMYS SCRIPTA*

Trachemys scripta elegans (Wied, 1839) is today, without doubt, the most widely distributed turtle in the world because of its popularity in the international pet trade. Its original range comprises the Mississippi valley and all its tributaries (New Mexico, Louisiana, Texas, Mississippi, Alabama, Oklahoma, Arkansas, Kansas, Tennessee and parts of Missouri, Indiana and Illinois). Small populations live naturally in Ohio and in the regions of Mexico adjoining Texas. Individuals have been introduced to many areas of the world and have often managed to survive and reproduce. Under conditions that are often unnatural or where the climate differs considerably from that of the original habitat, both eggs and hatchlings are quickly eliminated. Unfortunately, the widespread abandonment of young specimens in non-native natural surroundings may have an adverse effect on the native fauna and flora.

In its native environment, the turtle adapts to life in ponds and in the tranquil oxbows of rivers, where it can find plentiful vegetation. In other parts of the world, artificially introduced populations will inhabit virtually any natural or artificial body of water.

The carapace of older females of this subspecies may measure up to 28 cm (11 in) in length, whereas that of the males seldom exceeds 21 cm (8¼ in).

The typical red or orange-red marks on the sides of the head, often accompanied by an isolated patch positioned centrally on top of the head, constitute a criterion for immediate identification of this subspecies.

Very young specimens have a multicolored livery,

and the carapace is yellow-green with yellow spots and lines. This colorful design fades with growth and gives way to a uniformly olive to brown carapace or darkens to become almost black, especially in the males. Apart from being smaller than the females, the males are also distinguishable by the long claws of the forefeet and by the very long, sturdy tail.

The diet of the adults is predominantly vegetarian, while the young are almost exclusively carnivores, preying on small invertebrates.

The period of overwintering in original habitats, either on the bottom or submerged in the mud and detritus of stagnant water, extends from December to March.

Prior to mating, the male displays himself for hours to the female, lightly scraping his long foreclaws against her snout or gently nibbling at her neck, eventually mounting her back for copulation.

The female is prolific and may lay several clutches a year, each comprising 12 to 15 eggs. At a temperature of around 26°C (79°F), incubation lasts 50 to 60 days. In nature, this period is even longer, and the young, newly emerged from the egg, often spend the winter in the nest until the following spring. Growth of the young, too, is linked to temperature: the higher it is, the greater their size within the first few months.

The survival of original populations has been gravely jeopardized, due in part to the large-scale removal of individuals from their natural environment (in order to maintain a constant supply of salable specimens) and to the uncontrolled release of these animals into new surroundings. As a result, the species has been on the CITES list in Europe since December 1997, and its importation and sale is prohibited.

Distribution range of
Trachemys scripta.

T. s. scripta

T. s. troostii

T. s. elegans

T. s. gaigeae

T. s. cataspila

T. s. venusta

Facing page, an unusual picture shows the rapid growth rate in captivity of T. s. elegans. *Left, a specimen of* T. s. scripta.

Trachemys scripta scripta (Schoepff, 1792). Distributed from extreme southeastern Virginia, northern North Carolina, most of South Carolina, Georgia and northern Florida. It inhabits a wide variety of wet zones but does not form groups when basking. The males are smaller and have a less domed carapace than do the females. Individuals measure at most 28 cm (11 in) long. The area occupied by this species more or less overlaps that of the alligators, and hence the development of a strong carapace is an aid to defense. The plastron is pure yellow or with a black spot or ocellus on each gular scute. There is a large yellow streak and speckling behind either eye and large black marks on the lower part of each marginal scute. Clutches of 10 to 12 eggs are laid in May and June. The diet is omnivorous.

Trachemys scripta troostii (Holbrook, 1836). It is found in the upper reaches of the Cumberland and Tennessee Rivers and in neighboring zones. It also lives in channels and ponds. There is a thin yellowish stripe behind each eye and broader but fewer streaks below the chin; the plastron is bright yellow, with tiny black spots on the bridge. The carapace is smooth, without keels, measuring up to 28 cm (11 in) long. The young feed on small invertebrates, with more vegetation as they grow.

Above, a young albino specimen of Trachemys scripta elegans; *right, an adult of the same species; top right, the head of* Trachemys scripta troostii.

Desert tortoise
Gopherus agassizii (Cooper, 1863)

195

Family Testudinidae.

Distribution and habitat In the United States, in Nevada, Utah, California and Arizona; in Mexico, in Baja California, Sonora and Sinaloa.

Its habitats are subdesert zones, where it is found in oases, at the bottom of canyons and on rocky hillsides.

Characteristics The carapace, round and domed, has a maximum length of 50 cm (20 in). The forelimbs are heavily scaled and are used for digging deep burrows up to 10 m (33 ft) long, where it will seek refuge, often in groups, during the hottest periods. Courtship prior to coupling is fairly ritualized: Males move in a circle around the females, occasionally coming to a halt. They then test out their partners with nips to the head, foot and front of the plastron. If the female is receptive, she appears to join the "dance," likewise taking a few steps in a circle, pausing now and then and finally turning round to present the rear part of her shell to the male. Thus begins the attempt to mate, which, if not successful, leads to the pair repeating the procedure several times. The species lays 2 to 3 clutches annually, each comprising 2 to 14 eggs, which hatch in 90 to 120 days. Sexual maturity is reached at the age of about 20 years. A herbivore, the tortoise feeds on succulent plants.

Situation Listed in CITES Appendix II. Since 1990, the U.S. Fish and Wildlife Service (USFWS) has classified the species as threatened, and 14 reserves have been set up for its protection in the Mojave and Colorado Deserts. A conservation program also plans to move groups of these tortoises from either extremely arid zones or surroundings already subject to too much alteration and human interference to a suitable reserve (Desert Tortoise Natural Area).

Texas desert tortoise
Gopherus berlandieri (Agassiz, 1857)

Family Testudinidae.

Distribution and habitat Texas and in the regions of Cohauila, Nuevo León and Tamaulipas, Mexico. The species is found in a variety of habitats: whereas some populations in Texas frequent subtropical scrub forests, in Mexico, they are strictly localized in subdesert areas.

Characteristics The carapace is up to 22 cm (9 in) in length, with scutes that appear roughened as a result of conspicuous growth ridges. The gular scutes curve markedly forwards and away from the carapace. The tortoise does not dig burrows but often seeks shelter in the lairs of other animals; alternatively, with the aid of its gular scutes and strong claws, it scoops out a hollow in the midst of a tangle of a shrubs, where it returns to rest after its daily activities. There is a single annual clutch in June or July of 1 to 4 eggs. Predominantly herbivorous, it feeds primarily on succulent plants or cacti, although it also feeds on small insects and snails.

Situation Listed in CITES Appendix II. In spite of such protection, several thousand specimens are caught every year and traded; given its specialized habitat, it does not live long in captivity. Some breeders have set up collection centers for its readaptation to life in the wild.

Bolsan tortoise
Gopherus flavomarginatus (Legler, 1959)

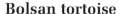

115

197

Family Testudinidae.

Distribution and habitat Mexico, in a fairly restricted area between the cities of Durango, Coahuila and Chihuahua, at altitudes of 1,000 to 1,300 m (3,300–4,300 ft). It lives in arid zones of steppe and sandy desert.

Characteristics The carapace, quite long and slightly domed, measures up to 37 cm (15 in) long. To escape extremes of temperatures, whether in summer or winter, it digs deep, long tunnels, where it will remain for months on end. Some of these galleries go down 2 m (6½ ft) and extend for more than 10 m (33 ft).

Mating occurs almost immediately after the partners make contact. Females lay 3 to 14 eggs twice a year, which hatch in approximately 100 days.

Food consists almost exclusively of fleshy, succulent plants.

Situation Listed in CITES Appendix I. The species is in fact gravely under threat because of its exceedingly hostile habitat and the low numerical density of known populations. Two special reserves have been set up for its protection: the Rancho Sombrereticco in Chihuahua and the Mapimí Reserve at Durango. In suitable areas, some

populations have been translocated under controlled conditions to zones that are less at risk.

In this and other *Gopherus* species, certain highly contagious bacterial infections, called upper respiratory tract infections (URTD) and caused by *Mycoplasma* spp., have been reported, with fatal outcomes for the victims.

Gopher tortoise
Gopherus polyphemus (Daudin, 1802)

Family Testudinidae.

Distribution and habitat Southern South Carolina and along the Atlantic coastal plain to Florida (excluding the everglades) and westward along the coastal plains of the Gulf to Louisiana. It lives in sandy, bushy zones and on prairies.

Characteristics The fairly long carapace measures around 30 cm (12 in). The tortoise reaches sexual maturity at the age of 16 to 21 years. To escape extremes of cold and hot temperature, this species excavates long burrows with a large terminal chamber, where it takes refuge. The opening of this cavity depends on the length of the carapace. Courtship and copulation follow the same sequence of phases as described for *Gopherus agassizii*. Females lay a single clutch of 5 to 9 eggs between April and July; hatching occurs in August and September. The species is vegetarian, with a preference for shoots and leaves, but sometimes eats insects or pieces of animal bone.

Situation Protected in CITES Appendix II, it is seriously threatened by the disappearance of its chosen habitats, which are progressively confined by human activity and the natural development of woodland cover. Conservation plans, in fact, entail the periodic cutting back of vegetation and the protection of principal sites. In the past, the tortoise was hunted for food, and today, it is still captured illegally in some regions for collections. Many specimens are killed by automobiles while attempting to cross the roads that divide their habitat.

Florida softshell turtle

Apalone ferox (Schneider, 1783)

Family Trionychidae.

Distribution and habitat Central eastern and southern United States. It is found in lakes, streams and rivers—even those that are deep and with a strong current—with a soft bed, where it can bury itself and lie in wait for prey, keeping only its snout close to the surface in order to breathe.

Characteristics The body may be up to 60 cm (2 ft). Like other species of the genus, it can "breathe" through the pharynx and anus thanks to the vascularized papillae in the mucus. It spends hours swimming or buried on the bottom.

The females lay a single annual clutch of 4 to 23 eggs, which incubate for up to 60 days.

The diet is omnivorous, but it prefers invertebrate prey such as mollusks and small fish.

Spiny softshell turtle
Apalone spinifera (Le Sueur, 1827)

Family Trionychidae.
Distribution and habitat It has been reported in Ontario and Quebec in

Canada and through much of the United States, from Vermont west to the Continental Divide and south to Mexico. Isolated populations in the Gila and Colorado Rivers in California, Nevada, Arizona and New Mexico. Over this range, seven subspecies have so far been described: *A. s. spinifera*, *A. s. asper*, *A. s. pallida*, *A. s. guadalupensis*, *A. s. emoryi*, *A. s. ater* and *A. s. hartwegi*. It may be found in almost all types of aquatic habitats but must be able to shelter on soft muddy or sandy bottoms and bask on adjoining banks.
Characteristics The round carapace has a rough leathery covering, with conical projections along the anterior edge of the

shell. It measures up to 50 cm (20 in) long.

Markedly aquatic, it spends much of the day hunting small prey on the bottom or floating on the surface; often it buries itself in the mud or sand, exposing only its neck and head so that it can reach the surface with the tip of its snout. The female probably lays more than 1 clutch from May to August, comprising 4 to 30 eggs; the young hatch in about 90 days, but in more northerly regions, they may delay emerging from the eggs until the following spring.

The diet is carnivorous, basically aquatic invertebrates, fish, amphibians and their larvae. It is the most popular of the Trionychidae species on the collectors' market and, for that reason, is widely bred in various countries outside their native lands. In Mexico, there have been initiatives to protect populations threatened with capture for food.

Smooth softshell turtle

Apalone mutica
(Le Sueur, 1827)

Family Trionychidae.

Distribution and habitat Central United States from Ohio, Minnesota and North Dakota south to Florida, Texas and New Mexico. There are two subspecies: *A. m. mutica* and *A. m. calvata*.

It lives in large rivers with a variable current, a soft bed and plenty of aquatic plants.

Characteristics The carapace is smooth and rounded, measuring up to 35 cm (14 in) in length, and is olive-green to orange-brown with dark spots. Very timid, the turtle seldom ventures ashore to bask. Mating takes place in the water, with eggs laid between May and July in chambers dug in the sandy banks or on river islets; there are 2 to 3 clutches a year of 10 to 20 eggs that hatch in 70 to 90 days.

The species is carnivorous, actively hunting aquatic invertebrates, amphibians and fish.

NEOTROPICAL REGION

NEOTROPICAL REGION

**Central America, West Indies,
Galápagos Islands and South America**

Such is the natural wealth of this region, it is thought that within the next 10 years, at least a million new animal species will be discovered in the Amazon basin alone and that these may include species of aquatic and semiaquatic turtles and tortoises. At the moment, however, the situation is bleak, because the progressive destruction of the rain forest and excessive hunting of turtles for their meat have threatened the survival of even the most widely distributed species (such as *Podocnemis expansa* and *P. unifilis*).

Only one family of Chelonia is found exclusively in this region: a genuine living fossil, Dermatemydidae, with its one known living species, *Dermatemys mawii*, which is found in large and small bodies of water in eastern Mexico, Guatemala and Belize. Yet the biogeographical distribution of the family Chelidae is of great interest, for it is found only in this region with five genera and in Australia and New Guinea; these Pleurodira, such as the very strange and gigantic matamata (*Chelus fimbriatus*) and the elegant *Phrynops* species, possess archaic features but are quite well distributed. The

*Previous spread, a scene of tranquillity as an Amazon river turtle (*Podocnemis unifilis*) basks in the warmth of the sun. Above, a typical Neotropical habitat. The long coastlines and solitary beaches of this region are a haven for marine turtles. Important breeding colonies of these ocean travelers (in particular, of* Dermochelys coriacea*) are to be found along the northern shores of Venezuela, French Guiana and Brazil.*

Neotropical region also takes in the southernmost limit and distribution of the Kinosternidae (with several species of *Kinosternon*, one of *Claudius* and two of *Staurotypus*), the Emydidae, with the genus *Trachemys*, and the Bataguridae, with *Rhinoclemmys*.

This region is also the home of various Testudinidae of medium and large dimensions: among the former are *Geochelone carbonaria* and *G. denticulata*; and among the latter is the famous giant Galápagos tortoise (*Geochelone nigra*). From the time of Darwin to the present day, the survival of these tortoises has been precarious due to the cruel and large-scale killing of these animals to provide fresh meat and combustible oil for 19th-century navigators and seamen; the predatory activities of many small and medium-size animals introduced to the islands by man; the extreme climatic conditions; and the devastating effects of repeated volcanic eruptions.

Certain anatomical features of the Dermatemydidae are very primitive, such as the presence of bony inframarginal plates on the carapace. The drawings show the appearance of the plastron (a) and carapace (b) of Dermatemys mawii.

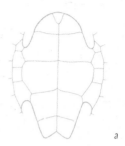

a

b

DERMATEMYDIDAE

There is fossil evidence of the family dating from the Cretaceous, but today, it is represented by a single species, *Dermatemys mawii*, a large aquatic turtle from Central America that very laboriously ventures onto land only during the breeding season.

Its aquatic way of life is facilitated by its ability to remain submerged for long periods by means of nasopharyngeal respiration of dissolved oxygen in the water. The carapace is broad and flat, and there are no claws on the feet.

Central American river turtle
Dermatemys mawii (Gray, 1847)

Family Dermatemydidae.
Distribution and habitat
Central southern Mexico, in the regions of Veracruz, Tabasco, Campeche, Chiapas and Quintana Roo; Guatemala and Belize. It lives in rivers, lakes, lagoons and temporary pools.
Characteristics The flattish olive-green carapace measures up to 65 cm (26 in). The turtle leads an almost wholly aquatic life and spends long periods of time underwater without reemerging.

The female lays 6 to 20 eggs twice a year in small chambers dug in the bank not far from the water.

The species is herbivorous, feeding principally on aquatic plants and ripe fruit fallen to the ground.
Situation The commercial demand for its meat is so heavy as to pose a serious threat to many populations of the species. It is listed in CITES Appendix II, but there are no local laws in force to prevent its large-scale capture.

Big-headed turtle
Peltocephalus dumerilianus (Schweigger, 1812)

Family Pelomedusidae.
Distribution and habitat Several rivers of the Amazon river basin and part of the Orinoco basin, in the South American countries of Colombia, Venezuela, Peru and Brazil.

It lives in the dark waters of rivers and streams and in stagnant pools.
Characteristics The oval, domed carapace may measure up to 68 cm (27 in) long. Clutches of 7 to 25 eggs are laid during the dry season; they hatch in approximately 100 days. The diet is omnivorous.

Llanos river turtle
Podocnemis vogli (Müller, 1935)

Family Pelomedusidae.
Distribution and habitat In the llanos of Venezuela and in Colombia. It is found mainly in rivers and isolated pools and ponds of the savanna.
Characteristics The oval, very flat carapace measures at most 36 cm (14¼ in) long.

The female, when ready to lay, will stray some miles from her usual habitat. There are 2 clutches annually, each of 5 to 20 elliptical eggs. The diet is omnivorous.
Situation Listed in CITES Appendix II because it is captured for food.

Arrau river turtle
Podocnemis expansa (Schweigger, 1812)

Family Pelomedusidae.
Distribution and habitat In the Orinoco, Essequibo and other rivers of the Amazon basin, from Colombia and Brazil to Bolivia; Trinidad.

It inhabits large rivers and deep waters, coming ashore only to bask, to find food and to reproduce.

Characteristics The carapace, much flattened and almost circular in shape, measures up to 100 cm (40 in) in length, making this the largest living *Podocnemis*. Females are bigger than males, weighing up to 50 kg (110 lb).

During the dry season, the turtles make their way toward extensive stretches of sand along the shores of lakes and rivers. Suitable nesting sites, few and far between, attract literally hundreds of reproductive adults, who court and mate continuously. At night, the female seeks out an appropriate nest location and excavates a flask-shaped nest up to 60 cm (2 ft) deep, in which she lays up to 100 spherical eggs. After a few weeks, all the turtles prepare to disperse—behavior that announces the arrival of rain. The diet is primarily herbivorous, based on aquatic plants, flowers, fruit and roots.

Situation Uncontrolled stealing of eggs has, within a few decades, brought about a serious reduction in numbers, persuading local governments to set up watches over breeding sites. In some parts of Venezuela (including Lake Valencia), the Management Plan for the Giant Amazonian Turtle has successfully established artificial nesting beaches. In Brazil, the Cenaqua/Ibama Program has released almost 17 million young turtles over a period of 13 years into the rivers of Amazonia. Listed in CITES Appendix II and considered an endangered species under the U.S.

Endangered Species Act and in the IUCN Amphibians and Reptiles Red Data Book (1996).

Aiaca turtle

Podocnemis sextuberculata
(Cornalia, 1849)

Family Pelomedusidae.
Distribution and habitat Amazon River in Brazil and the Putumayo and Caquetá Rivers in Colombia and Peru. Inhabits riverbanks, marshes and ponds. Another species, *Podocnemis erythrocephala* (Spix, 1824), is found in the same environments, typically distributed in the "blackwaters" of the Rio Negro but also in other tributaries of the Amazon, in eastern Colombia, in southern Venezuela and in northern Brazil.
Characteristics *P. sextuber-* *culata* is small: the carapace, which is broader at the rear, measures at most 32 cm (13 in) long. Nests are made in sandbars and beaches of rivers once or twice a year, where 8 to 19 elliptical eggs are laid (in *P. erythrocephala*, each clutch comprises 5 to 14 eggs). The diet is omnivo- rous and composed of directly caught fish and aquatic plants. The young catch small floating organisms.
Situation Both species are listed in CITES Appendix II and described in the IUCN Amphibian and Reptiles Red Data Book as "Insufficiently Known."

Family Pelomedusidae.
Distribution and habitat
In the Orinoco and other rivers of the Amazon basin, from Colombia to Brazil and Bolivia.

It lives in the same environments as *Podocnemis expansa* but also in fast-flowing rivers and lakes.
Characteristics The cara-

pace of older individuals measures up to 68.5 cm (27 in). An expert swimmer, this turtle takes advantage of periodic flooding to move to new surroundings. It does not travel such long distances or congregate in such large numbers as *P. expansa* at nesting sites during the breeding period (which coincides with seasonal low water). The females, separately from one another, lay 15 to 40 elongated eggs along the shores and sandbanks. The diet is mainly herbivorous, predominantly comprising leaves and roots, but it may also include aquatic

invertebrates or others that have fallen into the water.
Situation This is, of all *Podocnemis* species, the one most eagerly sought for its flesh, and even today, it is not uncommon to find it on sale in local markets. It is listed in CITES Appendix II, is regarded as "Endangered" under the U.S. Endangered Species Act, and "Vulnerable" in the IUCN Amphibians and Reptiles Red Data Book (1990). In Colombia, a project is under way, funded by the Fundación Natura di Bogotà to protect the Colombian Amazon populations.

Matamata
Chelus fimbriatus (Schneider, 1783)

Family Chelidae.

Distribution and habitat Northern part of South America, in Bolivia, Ecuador, Peru, Colombia, Venezuela, the Guyanas and Brazil. It lives in shallow blackwater streams with only a slight current, remaining for long periods half submerged in the muddy or sandy bottom, stretching out the head and neck to expose only the nostrils.

Characteristics The carapace alone may measure up to 45 cm (18 in), while the huge head may protrude another 20 cm (8 in). It is well camouflaged when motionless on the bottom, thanks to the texture of the carapace, with its rough ridges, and the presence of flaps of skin on the sides of the neck and head, which gives it the appearance of a rock encrusted with algae. Thus it can lie in wait to catch small fish and aquatic invertebrates.

The female lays a single yearly clutch of 10 to 30 eggs on the sandbanks.

Situation Large individuals are caught for their flesh. Many are captured for international collection traffic.

Snake-necked turtle

Hydromedusa tectifera (Cope, 1870)

Family Chelidae.

Distribution and habitat Southeastern regions of Brazil, eastern Paraguay, northern Argentina and Uruguay. It lives in all types of wet zones—in streams and rivers with a moderate current, a muddy bottom and plenty of aquatic vegetation and in ponds and pools.

Characteristics The oval, flat carapace measures up to 30 cm (12 in). The neck is extremely long, almost the length of the carapace, with many spiny tubercles. The females lay 2 to 5 elongated eggs. The diet is carnivorous.

Geoffroy's side-necked turtle

Phrynops geoffroanus (Schwrigger, 1814)

Family Chelidae.

Distribution and habitat It is found in a zone extending from Venezuela and Colombia to Paraguay and northern Argentina. There are two recognized subspecies: *P. g. geoffroanus* and *P. g. tuberosus*.

It lives in rivers, lakes and other bodies of water affording shelter among abundant aquatic vegetation.

Characteristics The oval, flat carapace measures up to 35 cm (14 in) in length. In juveniles, the pattern on the carapace is very elaborate, and the plastron is reddish with black spots.

The females lay 10 to 20 almost spherical eggs. The diet is carnivorous.

Situation A recovery program for the Brazilian populations has been set up at the breeding center of Brazil's São Paolo zoo. The species is still much in demand for collections, despite the great difficulty involved in rearing captive animals.

Gibba turtle
Phrynops gibbus (Schweigger, 1812)

Family Chelidae.
Distribution and habitat Widely distributed in northern and western South America. It lives in streams, rivers, pools and ponds within forests.
Characteristics The elliptical carapace, with a central keel, measures up to 23 cm (9 in) long.

Each female lays 2 to 4 eggs in holes, mounds of leaves or hollows among tree roots. These hatch after some 200 days' incubation. Omnivorous, it preys on small invertebrates, tadpoles and small fish.

Hilary's side-necked turtle
Phrynops hilarii (Duméril & Bibron, 1835)

Family Chelidae.
Distribution and habitat It is present over an area extending from central Brazil to Uruguay and Argentina, living in rivers and lakes but also in marshy zones and ponds with plenty of aquatic vegetation.

Characteristics The carapace may grow to a length of 40 cm (16 in). There are conspicuous black lines on the sides of the head. The female lays a dozen or so eggs once a year.

The diet is carnivorous, with an emphasis upon fish and mollusks.

Toad-headed turtle
Phrynops nasutus (Schweigger, 1814)

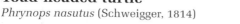

Family Chelidae.
Distribution and habitat Colombia, Peru, northern Bolivia and the Amazon basin of Brazil. It lives in lakes and ponds and in small pools in dense forest. The two species thus far described are *P. n. nasutus* and *P. s. wermuthi*.
Characteristics The carapace may grow to a length of 35 cm (14 in).

The female lays a single clutch annually that normally consists of 6 to 8 eggs.

The diet is carnivorous, comprising mainly small fish and aquatic invertebrates.

Twist-necked turtle
Platemys platycephala (Schneider, 1792)

Family Chelidae.
Distribution and habitat Northern South America, in river basins of Venezuela, Guyana, Bolivia, Ecuador, Peru, Colombia and Brazil. Two subspecies: *P. p. platycephala* and *P. p. melanonota*. It lives in shallow streams and stagnant pools.
Characteristics The elliptical, flat carapace is at most 18 cm (7 in). The species is associated with wet areas but does not remain long in the water. The females lay 1 egg a year, often on the ground. The diet is omnivorous.

Creaser's mud turtle
Kinosternon creaseri (Hartweg, 1934)

Family Chelidae.
Distribution and habitat
It is found only in the Yucatán Peninsula, in the Mexican states of Yucatán, Quintana Roo and Campeche. During the rainy season, it may frequent temporary pools in karstic zones; in the dry season, to avoid desiccation, it will estivate on the muddy bed.

Characteristics The length of the carapace of this species barely reaches 12 cm (5 in). There is a double hinge on the plastron that enables the turtle to shut itself in completely.

The female lays 1 to 2 large eggs several times a year. The species is territorial, and it is rare to find more than one adult male in a single pool.

Situation It is threatened by large-scale deforestation, which has long been occurring throughout Yucatán territory.

White-lipped mud turtle

Kinosternon leucostomum (Bibron & Duméril, 1851)

131

Family Kinosternidae.

Distribution and habitat From the state of Veracruz in Mexico, the range of this species extends to much of Central America and northern regions of South America.

The two recognized subspecies are *K. l. leucostomum* and *K. l. postinguinale*.

Quite comfortable on land, it lives in forest ponds, pools and streams, with a preference for stagnant water with plenty of aquatic vegetation. The Tabasco mud turtle, *Kinosternon acutum* (Gray, 1831), also lives on the plains of southern Mexico, from the regions of Veracruz to Chiapas, and in Belize and Guatemala.

Characteristics The carapace is oval, brownish black or black and about 18 cm (7 in) long; in the species *K. acutum*, it is at most 12 cm (5 in) in length.

A single keel is situated on the plastron between the abdominal and pectoral scutes. Little is known of its biology in the wild or of its reproductive behavior.

Its vast distribution and a constant temperate climate ensure that the species breeds throughout the year, with several clutches of 1 to 3 eggs. These are laid on the ground and promptly covered with a layer of leaves and other rotting plant matter, an environment well suited to incubation, which lasts 120 to 150 days.

With nocturnal habits and an omnivorous diet, the turtle seeks small prey in the water and eats parts of aquatic plants.

Situation Because of its small dimensions, the species is often sought for collections.

Narrow-bridged musk turtle
Claudius angustatus (Cope, 1865)

Family Kinosternidae.
Distribution and habitat Southern Mexico, from the state of Veracruz to Chiapas but excluding the Yucatán Peninsula; Guatemala and Belize. It lives in shallow water with a muddy bottom and an abundance of vegetation. To avoid desiccation, it will bury itself in the mud.

The species may belong, together with *Staurotypus*, to the family Staurotypidae.

Characteristics The oval carapace measures up to 16.5 cm (7 in) and is dark brown or brownish yellow with blackish tones. Individuals tend to be aggressive if threatened but generally manage to camouflage themselves, thanks to the growth of threadlike algae on the carapace.

The female may lay several annual clutches of 2 to 8 elongated eggs, which hatch in 110 to 150 days.

The diet is carnivorous: small aquatic invertebrates, fish and amphibians.

Mexican giant musk turtle
Staurotypus triporcatus (Weigmann, 1828)

Family Kinosternidae.
Distribution and habitat
Lowlands of southern Mexico, from Veracruz to Chiapas, with a limited presence in the Yucatán Peninsula; Guatemala, Belize and Honduras. Another species,

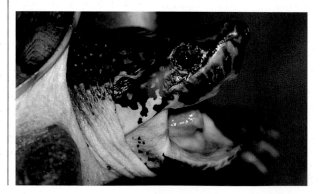

Staurotypus salvinii (Gray, 1864), is found from the Mexican states of Oaxaca and Chiapas to Guatemala and El Salvador. Habitats are medium and large bodies of slow-flowing water, as well as stagnant pools,

with abundant vegetation.
Characteristics The carapace measures up to 40 cm (16 in) long; it is oval, with three long, prominent keels. In *S. salvinii*, the maximum dimensions are around 25 cm (10 in), and the carapace is broader and flatter.

Both species are aggressive and are capable of defending their privacy with powerful bites. Their habits are almost exclusively aquatic.

The female of *S. triporcatus* lays a single clutch of 3 to 6 elliptical eggs during the year; *S. salvinii* have several clutches a year, each of up to 10 eggs. The diet is carnivorous.

Furrowed wood turtle
Rhinoclemmys areolata (Bibron & Duméril, 1851)

Family Bataguridae.
Distribution and habitat Central and eastern Mexico, in the states of Veracruz, Tabasco, Yucatán and Chiapas; parts of Belize, Guatemala and Honduras. Predominantly

terrestrial by habit, it is found in savannas and dense forests but also frequents wetter areas in the vicinity of marshes and ponds,

The Mexican spotted wood turtle, *Rhinoclem-*

mys rubida (Cope, 1870), is an inhabitant of plains and scrub woodland along the west coast of Mexico, from Jalisco to Oaxaca and southeastern Chiapas.
Characteristics The carapace measures up to 20 cm (8 in); that of *R. rubida* reaches 23 cm (9 in). The rear part of the female's carapace becomes flexible during the breeding period to facilitate the ejection of the large eggs, which are shaped much like birds' eggs. The diet is omnivorous but consists mainly of vegetation and fruit, supplemented by small invertebrates.

Spotted-legged turtle
Rhinoclemmys punctularia (Daudin, 1802)

135

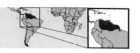

Family Bataguridae.
Distribution and habitat
South America from Colombia and Venezuela to the Guyanas and eastern Brazil, with three subspecies: *R. p. punctularia*, *R. p. diademata* and *R. p. flammigera*. It inhabits inland waters.
Characteristics The dark, domed carapace, up to 25 cm (10 in), is typically dark brown with light spots on the forelimbs and nape. Several times a year, the female lays 1 to 2 eggs among the roots of trees or in rotting leaves. The diet is omnivorous.

Antilles turtle
Trachemys decussata (Gray, 1831)

136

Family Emydidae.
Distribution and habitat
Various islands of the Antilles: Cuba, Piños, Grand Cayman and Cayman Brac. The two recognized subspecies are *T. d. decussata* and *T. d. angusta*. It lives in lowland streams and swamps with a sandy or muddy bottom and plenty of aquatic plants.
Characteristics The oval, slightly domed carapace measures up to 39 cm (16 in). As males age, they take on a blackish color on carapace and plastron.
The diet is herbivorous, especially among adults.

THE SUBSPECIES OF *TRACHEMYS SCRIPTA*

Trachemys scripta callirostris (Gray, 1855) is found in the Caribbean drainages of Colombia and Venezuela. An excellent swimmer, it frequents marshy zones and lagoons. The carapace measures up to 25 cm (10 in) long and is slightly depressed, oval in shape and bright green, each scute exhibiting a large black ocellus and several concentric yellow rings. With age, the color becomes more uniform and hazy. Mating takes place in deep but calm water, and clutches of 9 to 30 eggs are deposited in holes dug a short distance away. Incubation lasts 60 to 90 days. The diet is omnivorous, consisting mostly of small invertebrates, amphibians and mollusks. In Colombia, the subspecies is protected in an attempt to restrict the traffic in young and adults alike.

Trachemys scripta venusta (Gray, 1855) is distributed in Mexico, from the state of Veracruz to the whole Yucatán Peninsula. It lives in river estuaries and coastal lagoons and also in ponds of the Yucatán jungle. The carapace measures up to 48 cm (19 in) in length, each costal scute displaying large orange ocelli with a dark central spot. With age, the color may darken to black, but it is rare.

During the season, from January to April, up to 6 clutches of 12 to 20 eggs are laid at night on beaches and sandbanks.

The diet is omnivorous, adults being herbivores for the most part. Because the subspecies is hunted excessively for food, it is nowadays quite rare throughout its range.

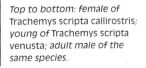

Top to bottom: female of Trachemys scripta callirostris; *young of* Trachemys scripta venusta; *adult male of the same species.*

Yellow-footed tortoise
Geochelone denticulata (Linnaeus, 1766)

Family Testudinidae.
Distribution and habitat
Southern Venezuela to Peru and Bolivia, with a very scattered, discontinuous range. It is found

in tropical evergreen forests and deciduous rain forests.

Characteristics This is the largest species of land tortoise in the mainland

zone of South America; the elongated carapace may measure up to 82 cm (32 in). The anterior surfaces of the forelimbs are covered with yellow or orange scales.

The female lays 6 to 7 clutches, more or less, throughout the year, each consisting of 4 to 8 elongated eggs that hatch in 120 to 150 days. The diet is herbivorous.

Situation Listed in CITES Appendix II. The species is locally threatened by alterations to its habitats and by being hunted for food.

Red-footed tortoise
Geochelone carbonaria (Spix, 1824)

223

Family Testudinidae.

Distribution and habitat Central and South America, from Panama and Colombia, through Venezuela and Brazil (except for the Amazon basin) to several Caribbean islands; in Guyana, Surinam, French Guiana, Bolivia, Paraguay and Argentina. It lives in open zones of wet savannas and tropical forests.

Characteristics The long, sturdy carapace, measuring up to 51 cm (20 in), is blackish; the vertebral and pleural scutes have broad

yellowish or reddish orange greolae.

Females lay 2 to 15 elongated eggs several times a year. The diet is herbivorous, basically made up of succulent plants, grasses and cacti.

Situation Listed in CITES Appendix II. The tortoise is widely captured for food and for the international traffic in pet animals. In Colombia, a breeding center was established in 1998 for the conservation and future welfare of the species.

Chilean tortoise
Geochelone chilensis (Gray, 1870)

Family Testudinidae.
Distribution and habitat
Bolivia, Paraguay and Argentina and south to the northern part of Patagonia. It lives on dry plains such as tree savannas (as in the photograph), shrubby zones and subdesert areas.

Characteristics The carapace is oval, dorsally flattened, up to 43 cm (17 in) long.

The female lays 1 to 6 eggs 2 or 3 times a year, with an incubation period of more than 125 days.

The diet is herbivorous, consisting mainly of leaves and grass seeds, but supplemented by fruit and berries.

Situation Listed in CITES Appendix II. It is caught for its flesh and as a potential pet in various parts of its range. In Argentina, for example, despite the existence of protective laws, it is reckoned that in the two provinces of Córdoba and Santiago del Estero alone, from 20,000 to 50,000 specimens are caught and transported to Buenos Aires.

THE GIANT TORTOISES OF THE GALÁPAGOS ISLANDS

Among the earliest chelonians were a number of giant forms, mainly with marine lifestyles, such as the aforementioned *Archelon* of the Cretaceous, which measured more than 3 m (10 ft) in length. But gigantism in terrestrial forms appeared much later, judging from fossils. Several Pliocene deposits in India have revealed the remains of a giant tortoise with a carapace measuring some 2.5 m (8 ft) long, classified as *Colossochelys atlas*.

During the Pliocene and Pleistocene, the phenomenon was not uncommon among various groups of animals. Only on certain small islands in the Pacific and Indian Oceans, however,

were some forms of giant tortoises able to evolve and survive until the present day, thanks to their environmental isolation and the absence of predators and food competitors (since they were essentially herbivores).

Human intervention, however, in the form of unrestricted hunting and the introduction of non-native animals to the habitats of these tortoises, brought these huge animals to actual or near extinction on certain islands, notably the Seychelles, Mauritius and the Galápagos archipelago in the Pacific Ocean.

The giant tortoises of the Indian Ocean were discovered in

Facing page, typical habitat of Geochelone chilensis.

the 16th century, but it was only with the first permanent human settlement on Mauritius (by the Dutch in 1638) that the animals were caught and used as food. Subsequently, the tortoises were freely captured and traded among the islands.

In 1840, the endemic species of Mauritius, Réunion, Rodriguez and Mahé were considered to be extinct.

Because their capture was

Above, a female of Geochelone nigra nigra *from Indefatigable Island. Right, at the peak moment of mating, the male emits clearly audible cries. The fertilized females then make for their egg-laying sites, which may be several hundred yards away.*

prohibited in 1891, the present population on the Aldabra atoll fortunately survived. The species *Geochelone gigantea* was also saved due to the extremely isolated position of the atoll, far from the most frequented shipping lanes.

On the Galápagos Islands, 15 subspecies of *Geochelone nigra*, commonly known as the giant Galápagos tortoise, were differentiated—almost one per island. Because of some three centuries of indiscriminate and deliberate capture by seamen who hunted the tortoises for their fat, which was rendered into oil, only 12 have survived to the present day.

Another reason these subspecies became extinct or very rare was the colonists' introduction to the islands of various predatory animals and food competitors, such as rats, dogs, cats, pigs, goats and donkeys.

Above, the only living example of the subspecies Geochelone nigra abingdonii *on Abingdon Island.*

In 1959, the islands were converted into a national park by the government of Ecuador, and since 1965, the Tortoise Rearing Program has been breeding these tortoises and repatriating them into their natural habitat. Indeed, most of the conservation initiatives undertaken concern the subspecies whose numbers are greatly reduced and those threatened by the frequent volcanic eruptions on some of the islands.

Above, three adults of Geochelone nigra *take a dip in a rare water puddle.*

NEOTROPICAL REGION

227

Giant Galápagos tortoise
Geochelone nigra (Quoy & Gaimard, 1824)

Family Testudinidae.
Distribution and habitat
It is present only in the Galápagos archipelago, Ecuador. The physical variability of these huge tortoises, which were found on the different islands but stemmed from a common ancestor, was among the examples taken by Charles Darwin to prove his theory of evolution. The difference between the several known forms of *Geochelone nigra* is in fact limited to the nomenclature of the subspecies concerned and is today very confusing and much debated.

The recognized forms, therefore, are: *G. n. abingdonii* (Pinta/Abingdon Island), *G. n. chathamensis* (San Cristóbal/Chatham Island), *G. n. darwinii* (San Salvador/James Island), *G. n. hoodensis* (Española/Hood Island), *G. n. phantastica* (Fernandina/Narborough Island), *G. n. ephippium* (Pinzon/Duncan Island), *G. n. microphyes* (Isabela/Albermarle Island), *G. n. vicina* (Isabela/Albermarle Island), *G. n.*

galapagoensis (Isabela/Albermarle Island), *G. n. nigrita* (Santa Cruz/Indefatigable Island), *G. n. vandenburghi* (Isabela/Albermarle Island). *G. n. abingdonii* survives with a single male specimen at Charles Darwin Station on the island of Santa Cruz. Of the subspecies *G. n. phantastica*, the last report of a living specimen was in 1906.

For the subspecies *G. n. hoodensis*, a recovery program was begun in 1965. From the initial 14 individuals (12 females and 2 males), it proved possible by 1975 to reintroduce to the wild 700 tortoises born in captivity; and in 1990,

the freed population began to reproduce.

The living environments are varied: some islands are entirely flat without relief, while others show their volcanic origins; some have luxuriant vegetation, whereas others are arid, dotted only with cacti. The tortoises are often observed making seasonal migrations from one habitat to another, according to rainfall, temperature or availability of food.

Characteristics The carapace of the biggest males of the largest subspecies may measure 150 cm (5 ft) but the average length is around 100 cm (3¼ ft). Carapace, plastron and the

rest of the body are black, and there is no nuchal scute on the carapace. The females choose suitable sites on soft ground for laying their 4 to 10 eggs, which hatch after 120 to 210 days. The diet is herbivorous, with adaptations in some forms to include the thorny stems and fruits of an indigenous cactus, *Opuntia arborea*, the only food opportunity offered by certain islands.

Situation The entire group is listed in CITES Appendix I.

Below, a closeup of the sole surviving member of Geochelone nigra abingdonii, known simply as Lonesome George.

AUSTRALIAN REGION

AUSTRALIAN REGION

New Guinea, Australia, Tasmania, New Zealand, New Guinea, New Caledonia, Melanesia, Micronesia and Polynesia

The species of aquatic and semiaquatic turtles in this region are concentrated along the final land outposts of Asia (Timor, Celebes) and in New Guinea and north-eastern Australia. Meanwhile, the multitude of islands and atolls scattered through the Pacific Ocean provide temporary breeding sites and feeding areas (the surrounding shores and coral reefs) for certain marine turtles such as *Natator depressa* and *Chelonia mydas agassizii*. One exception to this distribution is the Hawaiian archipelago, where, over the course of decades of Western colonization, various Asiatic and North American species have been introduced (e.g., *Pelodiscus sinensis* among the Trionychidae and *Trachemys scripta* among the Emydidae).

The geographical isolation of the Australian region has encouraged the survival of archaic forms, such as the Chelidae (though also represented by genera in South America), as well as uniquely strange forms, such as the Carettochelyidae. There is still much to be discovered about the animal life in this region (e.g., Papua New Guinea), and it is reasonable to suppose that new species may still be discovered. In fact, the discovery of new species of Australian Chelidae has stimulated lively debate about the taxonomic identity of the genera *Elseya* and *Emydura*. The present-day habitats are for the most part situated in areas that are thus far little disturbed by human activity, and for this reason, almost all species are naturally protected. Australian legislation has for some time provided for the safeguarding of local wildlife, prohibiting hunting and capture and imposing strict controls on commerce. Only *Pseudemydura umbrina* and *Rheodytes leukops*, strongly localized and highly specialized, remain under threat.

232

Previous spread, the imposing silhouette of Ayers Rock, sacred mountain of the Australian aborigines, resembles the shell of a gigantic turtle.

The vast expanses of sparsely populated, extremely dry terrain of central Australia, top, and the great rivers and swamplands of the northeastern zones, above, are favored habitats of the Chelidae.

Pig-nose turtle
Carettochelys insculpta (Ramsay, 1887)

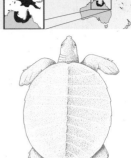

CARETTOCHELYIDAE

Fossil remains suggest that this family first appeared in the Eocene; nowadays, it is represented by one living species with unique characteristics. It possesses, in fact, flipperlike forelimbs like that of a marine turtle; the absence of horny scutes on the carapace, which is covered with thick, leathery skin, and the shape of the snout, with the nostrils positioned at the tip, liken it to a member of the Trionychidae. These anatomical adaptations make the species an agile swimmer (it lives in inland waters, brackish or fresh water), either in shallow swamp zones or in the final reaches of swift-flowing watercourses. Except during the breeding season, the turtle seldom ventures ashore, but it may bask on floating objects. Because hardly anything is known of its range, even its biology in the wild remains something of a mystery. It is locally (Papua) threatened with capture for food and for the collectors' market.

Family Carettochelyidae.
Distribution and habitat Rivers of Papua New Guinea and Northern Territory of Australia. It leads an extremely aquatic life in rivers, lakes and lagoons.
Characteristics The carapace, grayish or olive-green, may measure up to 55 cm (22 in) in length; it has a leathery, granular surface with smooth edges; in the young, there is a pronounced vertebral keel, and the border on the carapace is serrated.

Females come ashore to lay eggs during the night; each clutch is composed of 13 to 15 eggs,
The diet is omnivorous, based on aquatic plants, ripe fruit, water insects and small fish.
Situation Because of its appearance and characteristics, it often features in terrariums and aquariums.

233

CHELIDAE

This is the second family of the Pleurodira, distributed both in South America east of the Andes chain, with the genera *Chelus, Acantochelys, Phrynops, Platemys* and *Hydromedusa*, and in the Australian region with the genera *Emydura, Pseudemydura, Elseya, Chelodina* and *Rheodytes*. The skeleton of the shell and head is more highly evolved than that of the Pelomedusidae—for example, the mesoplastral bones are wholly absent, and the cervical vertebrae have a different type of joint—and the form of neck is unique, in some species extremely elongated, which explains the common name of side-necked turtles (*Chelodina*).

Identifying the genera of present-day Chelidae

1. *Flattened, triangular head, with the two parts of the lower jaw not welded together in the middle; numerous threadlike scales and free flaps of skin on neck; (d) tip of snout terminates in a tubular nasal structure →* Chelus.

1a. *Head not much flattened, without scales except for simple barbels on chin; tip of snout not tubelike →* 2.

2. *Extremely elongated neck, often the length of the carapace (e) →* 3.

2a. *Neck much shorter than carapace →* 4.

3. *Nuchal scute very broad, but separated from front edge of carapace by central part of contiguous marginal scutes; (a) 6 to 9 neural bones present; large intergular scute completely separating gular scutes →* Hydromedusa.

3a. *Nuchal scute not separated from front edge of carapace; (b) neural bones absent (except in* Chelodina *oblonga); intergular scute does not completely separate (c) gular scutes →* Chelodina.

4. *Very broad intergular scute, which completely separates gular, humeral and, in part, pectoral scutes; top edge of skull slightly notched →* Pseudomydura.

4a. *Small intergular scute, which completely separates gular scutes and, only partially, the humeral scutes →* 5.

5. *Neural bones present; top edge of skull extensively notched (f) →* Phrynops.

5a. *Neural bones absent →* 6.

6. *First vertebral scute not particularly large (narrower*

Above, two pictures of members of the Elseya spp. Apart from the huge matamata of South America (Chelus fimbriatus) and the snake-necked turtles of Australia (Chelodinae subspecies), the family of Chelidae is not widely known. Some species, however, are conspicuous for their handsome pattern (such as Phrynops geoffroanus) or for exceptional biological features (as, for example, the "cloacal breathing" of Rheodytes leukops).

than the second); symphysis of lower jaw wider than diameter of eye socket → 8.

6a. First vertebral scute much broader than second vertebral scute; symphysis of lower jaw narrower than diameter of eye socket → 7.

7. Rear part of head covered by single large scale; erect tubercles present on upper part of neck → Elseya.

7a. Rear part of head covered by smooth skin; blunt tubercles present on upper part of neck (h) → Emydura.

8. Carapace with deep medial groove → 9.

8a. Carapace with shallow medial groove → Rheodytes.

9. Shallow medial groove; back of head covered by small scales → Acanthochelys.

9a. Deep central groove, edged with a visible ridge of carapace; back of head without scales (i) → Platemys.

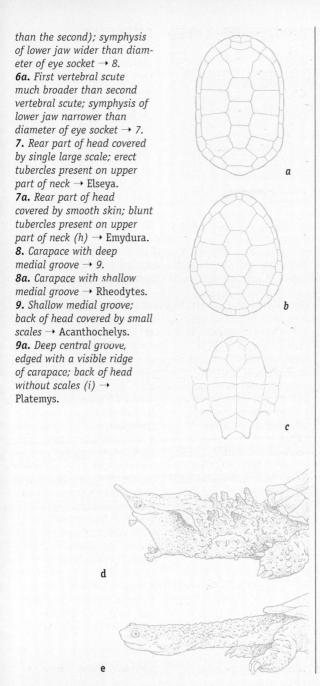

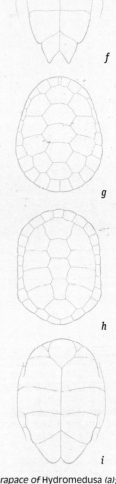

Carapace of Hydromedusa (a); carapace of Chelodina (b); plastron of Chelodina (c); head and neck of Chelus (d); head and neck of Chelodina (e); plastron of Phrynops (f); carapace of Emydura (g); carapace of Platemys (h); plastron of Platemys (i).

Giant snake-necked turtle
Chelodina expansa (Gray, 1857)

142

Family Chelidae.
Distribution and habitat Australia (Queensland and New South Wales). It lives in streams and rivers, even with a strong current.
Characteristics The very long neck measures up to two-thirds the length of the carapace, which may reach 48 cm (19 in), making it the largest Australian species of the Chelidae. Females lay 3 to 4 clutches of 5 to 25 eggs in the wet seasons, with an incubation period of 200 to 400 days. Carnivorous, it hunts small fish, amphibians and insects.

236

Rotti snake-necked turtle
Chelodina mccordi (Rhodin, 1994)

143

Family Chelidae.
Distribution and habitat This species has only recently been judged as distinct from *C. novaeguineae*. It lives only on the island of Rotti, near Timor, while the other species is found in southeastern New Guinea and northern regions of Australia (Queensland and Northern Territory). Its habitats are streams and ponds.
Characteristics The carapace may grow to a length of 30 cm (12 in). Females lay clutches of 9 to 21 eggs, which incubate after 60 days. Omnivorous.

Australian snake-necked turtle
Chelodina longicollis (Shaw, 1802)

144

Family
Chelidae.
**Distribution
and habitat** It
can be found
throughout east-
ern Australia, liv-
ing in slow-flowing

rivers, marsh-
es, ponds
and lagoons.
It prefers to
position itself
in shallow
water.
Characteristics The

extremely long neck is
more than two-thirds the
length of the carapace,
which itself measures up
to 28 cm (11 in).

Mating takes place in
September and October,
with eggs being laid some
two months later. Females
lay only 1 clutch annually
of 6 to 20 eggs, which incubate for 120 to 150 days.

The species is carnivo-
rous and may catch fish,
amphibians and other
aquatic invertebrates.
Situation This is the most
common and popular of
the Chelidae species for
private breeding, and many
individuals successfully
reproduce in captivity.

Siebenrock's snake-necked turtle
Chelodina siebenrocki (Werner, 1901)

145

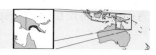

Family Chelidae.
Distribution and habitat South coast of New Guinea, in tidal areas of streams, lagoons and coastal swamps.
Characteristics The carapace is very dark, often blackish, up to 30 cm (12 in) long. The plastron is yellow or light brown, sometimes with dark streaks. The 4 to 17 elongated eggs are laid at the end of the wet season (May) and hatch after some 180 days. A carnivore, it hunts insects and other aquatic invertebrates.

Steindachner's turtle
Chelodina steindachneri (Siebenrock, 1914)

146

Family Chelidae.
Distribution and habitat Western Australia in seasonal watercourses linked to rainfall. During the dry periods, it buries itself on the bottom.
Characteristics The carapace is flattened, almost round in shape, measuring about 21 cm (8¼ in) in length. Little is known of its biology. The diet is carnivorous, comprising mainly invertebrates and fish.

Australian snapping turtle
Elseya dentata (Gray, 1836)

Family Chelidae.
Distribution and habitat Throughout northern and eastern Australia (Northern Territory and Queensland). It lives in rivers, swampy zones and ponds.
Characteristics The flattened oval carapace is grayish to dark brown, with rough scutes, and measures up to 40 cm (16 in) in length. The female lays 3 to 5 eggs once a year, which hatch after 180 days. The diet is omnivorous, based mainly on small invertebrates, fish and aquatic plants.

239

Saw-shelled snapping turtle
Elseya latisternum (Gray, 1867)

Family Chelidae.
Distribution and habitat The Cape York Peninsula to New South Wales, in streams, rivers, marshes and lagoons.
Characteristics The carapace is oval, the posterior edge markedly serrated, olive-green or grayish brown and up to 28 cm (11 in) long. The females lay several clutches a year, each with 9 to 17 elongated eggs. The diet is opportunistic, mainly carnivorous. It defends itself by snapping and emitting a foul smell from the musk glands.

New Guinea snapping turtle
Elseya novaeguineae (Meyer, 1874)

Family Chelidae.
Distribution and habitat It is found throughout New Guinea in small and moderate watercourses, in coastal swamps and in ponds.
Characteristics The carapace is oval and rounded, brownish or blackish and up to 30 cm (12 in) long. The back of the head is covered by a large horny scale. The female lays 5 to 20 eggs. The diet is opportunistic, prevalently carnivorous.

240

Murray River turtle
Emydura macquarri (Gray, 1831)

Family Chelidae.
Distribution and habitat Southeastern Australia, Queensland and South Australia, in streams and rivers, including those with a strong current. The species was formerly known as *Emydura australis*.
Characteristics The carapace is oval and brownish, and up to 30 cm (12 in). Mating occurs in the water, with plastron against plastron. The females lay 7 to 15 eggs, which hatch after some 80 days. The diet is primarily carnivorous, consisting mostly of aquatic mollusks.

Red-bellied short-necked turtle
Emydura subglobosa (Krefft, 1876)

151

241

Family Chelidae.
Distribution and habitat Southern New Guinea and northeastern Australia, on Cape York Peninsula and Queensland. With strong aquatic habits, it emerges onto the shores of the lakes and rivers only to bask and to lay eggs.

Characteristics The carapace, with an average length of 18 to 23 cm (8–9 in), is charcoal gray, without patterns; the plastron and bridge are a lighter, shiny gray. The head is gray or olive, with a yellow stripe running from the tip of the snout to behind each eye. The neck has reddish streaks. The female lays 7 to 14 eggs at night in a hole excavated very rapidly a short distance from the water. The young hatch in characteristic manner: they use their "egg tooth," a horny projection located at the tip of the hatchlings' snout, to peck out a small opening in the egg. The species is omnivorous, hunting small invertebrates.
Situation In Australia, it is protected; but there is a steady export traffic from New Guinea.

Western swamp turtle
Pseudemydura umbrina (Siebenrock, 1901)

152

Family Chelidae.
Distribution and habitat
It lives in a very constricted area of southwestern Australia (near the city of Perth),

flourishing in seasonal pools and swamps, which dry up completely during the summer, in the Bullbrook and Swan regions.

Together with *Chelodina oblonga*, it is an example of an endemic species that has adapted perfectly to a local arid climate.

Characteristics The carapace is almost rectangular, flattened and sunken longitudinally and brown to black in color. It measures only 14 cm (5½ in) long, the smallest of the Chelidae species. The egg-laying process is drawn out over some two months, starting in November, and the 3 to 5 eggs hatch after approximately 180 days.

The diet is for the most part carnivorous, based on small aquatic prey (fish, amphibians, insects and their larvae) but largely supplemented by vegetable matter.

Situation This is the most localized and rare Australian turtle species (the natural population is estimated at only 100 or so individuals, with a further 160 in captivity). For this species, the main threats come from fire outbreaks in the summer months that kill the reptiles on land during their estivation period and from the entire alteration of the majority of their original habitats as they are converted for agricultural, industrial or urban purposes.

The species is protected from capture for collections, thanks to its listing in CITES Appendix I and apposite Australian regulations. Two special reserves have been set up near Perth, at Ellen Brook and at Twin Swamps. An intensive breeding program operates at the Perth zoo. The Australian government also plans to finance the acquisition of areas close to the Ellen Brook reserve.

The swampy zones of south-western Australia, below, which are home to Pseudemydura umbrina, *are enclaves in the midst of extremely arid regions.*

Fitzroy River turtle
Rheodytes leukops
(Legler & Cann, 1980)

Family Chelidae.
Distribution and habitat

This Australian species is found only in the Fitzroy River basin in the state of Western Australia. It frequents well-oxygenated reaches of the river and its tributaries, living on the sandy or pebbly bottom, near places on shore where it can bask.

Characteristics The carapace is elliptical, the rear part serrated to varying extent (more so in young specimens), and measures up to 26 cm (10¼ in) long.

Dissolved oxygen in the water is fully exploited by gaseous exchange through the internal cloacal mucus. Up to 5 annual clutches have been observed, each of 40 to 50 eggs, which are very small and elongate. The eggs hatch after about 50 days. The diet is carnivorous, consisting mainly of small invertebrates.

APPENDICES

The index lists the species of turtles and tortoises thus far described and classified. Families are shown in bold lettering, while the subspecies, where mentioned, follow the species to which they belong. The biogeographical regions where they are found are indicated thus: OCEA = Seas and-oceans; PALE = Palearctic subregion; AFRI = Afrotropical region; ORIE = Oriental region; NEAR = Nearctic subregion; NEOT = Neotropical region; AUST = Australian region. The numbers that follow indicate the page or pages of the individual entry or mentions elsewhere in the book.

Arnold, E. N. and Burton, J.A., 1978—*A Field Guide to the Reptiles and Amphibians of Britain and Europe.* Collins, London. 272 pp.

Baillie, J. and Groombridge, B. (eds), 1996—*1996 IUCN Red List of Threatened Animals.* IUCN, Gland. 368 pp.

Ballasina, D., 1995—*Salviamo le tartarughe.* Edagricole Bologna, European Commission. RANA International Foundation. 260 pp.

Ballasina, D., 1995—*Red Data Book of Mediterranean Chelonians.* Edagricole, Bologna, European Commission. RANA International Foundation. 190 pp.

Baur, G., 1890—*On the Classification of the Testudinata.* Amer. Natur., 24; 530–536.

Bjorndal, K. A. (ed.), 1981—*Biology and Conservation of Sea Turtles.* Smithsonian Institution Press, Washington, D.C. 583 pp.

Boulenger, G. A., 1889—*Catalogue of the Chelonians, Rhynchocephalians and Crocodiles in the British Museum (Natural History).* Taylor and Francis, London. 311 pp.

Bruno, S., 1973—*Problemi di conservazione nel campo dell'erpetologia.* Atti III Simposio Nazionale Conservaz. Natura, Bari.

Bruno, S., 1986—*Tartarughe e Sauri d'Italia.* Giunti, Florence.

Carr, A. F. Jr., 1952—*Handbook of Turtles. The Turtles of the United States, Canada, and Baja California.* Cornell University Press, Ithaca, New York. 542 pp.

Conant, R., 1958, 1975—*A Field Guide to Reptiles and Amphibians of Eastern and Central North America.* Houghton Mifflin, Boston. 429 pp.

Di Palma, M. G. et al, 1989—*Indagini sulla ovodeposizione di Caretta caretta (L. 1758) in Sicilia.* Naturalista sicil., IV, XIII. 53–59.

Di Tizio, L., 1992—*Tartarughe palustri.* Vallecchi Edit., Florence. 72 pp.

Duguy, R., 1983—*La Tortue Luth (Dermochelys coriacea) sur les Côtes de France.* Ann. Soc. Scienc. Natur. de la Charente-Maritime.

Duméril, A. M. C. and Bibron, G., 1835—*Erpétologie générale, ou histoire naturelle complète des reptiles. Vol. 2.* Librairie Encyclopédique, Paris. 680 pp.

Ernst, C. H. and Barbour, R. W., 1989 — *Turtles of the World.* Smithsonian Institution Press, Washington, D.C. 313 pp.

Ferri, V., 1992—*Tartarughe terrestri e acquatiche.* De Vecchi Editore, Milan. 159 pp.

Gauthier, J., Estes, R. and De Queiroz, K., 1988—*The Early Evolution of the Amniota,* in Benton, M. G. (ed.), *The Phylogeny and Classification of the Tetrapods, Vol. 1: Amphibians, Reptiles, Birds.* Clarendon Press, Oxford. 103–155.

Gray, J. E., 1831—*Synopsis Reptilium or Short Descriptions of the Species of Reptiles. Pt. 1. Cataphracta, Tortoises, Crocodiles and Enaliosaurians.* London. 85 pp.

Gray, J. E., 1855—*Catalogue of Shield Reptiles in the Collections of the British Museum, 1. Testudinata (Tortoises).* Taylor and Francis, London, 79 pp.

Gray, J. E., 1870—*Supplement to the Catalogue of Shield Reptiles in the Collection of the British Museum. Pt. 1. Testudinata (tortoises).* Taylor and Francis, London, 120 pp.

Gray, J. E., 1872—*Notes on the Mud-tortoises of India (Trionyx geoffroyi),* Ann. Mag. Natur. Hist. (London) (4) 10: 326–340.

Harless, M. and Morlock, H., 1979—*Turtles: Perspectives and Research.* John Wiley & Sons, New York, 695 pp.

Hediger, H., 1964—*Wild Animals in Captivity. An Outline of the Biology of Zoological Gardens.* Dover Public. Inc., New York.

IUCN, 1971—*Marine Turtles: Proceedings of the Second Working Meeting of Marine Turtle Specialists.* Morges, Switzerland.

King, Wayne F. and Burke, R. L., 1997—*Turtle, Tuatara, Crocodile Checklist.* Association of Systematics Collections.

Kuhn, O., 1976—*Encyclopedia of Paleoherpetology,* Gustav Fischer Verlag, Stuttgart.

Mortimer, J., 1984—*Marine Turtles in the Republic of the Seychelles, Status and Management:* Report on project 1809 (1981–1984). IUCN Conservation Library, Cambridge.

National Audubon Society, 1979—*Field Guide to North American Reptiles and Amphibians.* A. A. Knopf, New York.

Nutaphand Wirot, 1979—*The Turtles of Thailand. Siam Farm Zoological Garden.* Mitbandung Press, Bangkok. 222 pp.

Obst, F. J. and Meusel, W., 1969—*Die Landschildkroten Europas und der Mittelmeerländer.* A. Ziemsen Verlag, Wittenberg Lutherstadt. 67 p.

Pritchard, P. C. H., 1967—*Living Turtles of the World.* T. F. H. Publications Inc., Jersey City, New Jersey. 288 pp.

Pritchard, P. C. H. and Rhodin, A. G. J. (eds), 1997—*The Conservation Biology of Freshwater Turtles, 1. Old World Turtles. 2. New World Turtles.* IUCN/SSC Tortoise and Freshwater Turtles Specialist Group.

Siebenrock, F., 1909 — *Synopsis der Rezenten Schildkröten, mit Berücksichtigung der in Historischer Zeit Ausgestorbenen Arten.* Zool. Jahrb., suppl., 10: 427–618.

Stubbs, D., 1989—*Tortoise and Freshwater Turtles: an Action Plan for Their Conservation.* IUCN Species Action Plans, Cambridge.

Swingland, I. R. and Klemens, M. W., 1989—*The Conservation Biology of Tortoises.* IUCN Species Survival Commission, Cambridge.

Various authors, 1971—*Proceedings of the second Working Meeting of Marine Turtle Specialists,* IUCN 8–10 March 1971, Morges, Switzerland. IUCN Publications New Series. 108 pp.

Various authors, 1995—*Proceeding of International Congress of Chelonian Conservation,* France, Gonfaron, Tortoise Village, 6–10 July, 1995. Edit. Soptom. 344 pp.

Various authors, *Proceedings: Conservation, Restoration and Management of Tortoises and Turtles. An International Conference.* A Joint Publication of the New York Turtle and Tortoise Society and WCS Turtle Recovery Program. xxiv 494 pp.

Watson, D. M. S., 1914—*Eunotosaurus africanus Seeley and the Ancestors of the Chelonia.* Proceeding Zoological Society, London, 2: 1011–1020.

Wermuth, H. and Mertens, R., 1961—*Schildkröten, Krocodile, Bruchenechsen.* G. Fischer Verlag, Jena. 422 pp.

WWF TRAFFIC ITALIA, 1989—*Manuale contro il commercio illegale di animali e piante selvatiche.*

Zunnino, M. and Zullino, A., 1995—*Biogeografia. La dimensione spaziale dell'evoluzione.* Casa Ed. Ambrosiana. Milan. 310 pp.

amnion *Protective membrane enveloping embryo in eggs of reptiles, birds and mammals.*

anapsid *Primitive arrangement of the bony roof that forms the skull of vertebrates, without lateral openings, retained only by the Chelonia.*

anoxia *Deficient supply of oxygen in the tissues.*

areole *Central and top part of the horny scales or laminae that cover the shell of the Chelonia.*

bony plates *Layered structures that provide internal support in the skeletal system of the Chelonia.*

box turtle *Popular name for turtles that can close their shell like a box, thanks to the mobility of parts of the plastron.*

bridge *More or less bony juncture point of the plastron and the carapace.*

carapace *Upper and back part of the bony shell of the Chelonia.*

chelonian *Member of the order Chelonia, which comprises extinct and living tortoises and turtles.*

cloaca *Common chamber into which the intestinal, urinary and reproductive tracts empty their contents, opening to the outside through the anus.*

cooter *Popular name for the pond turtles of the genus Chrysemys.*

dormancy *Period of inactivity during the coldest months or in adverse climatic conditions.*

endoskeleton *Internal skeleton as found in vertebrates.*

estivation *Period of dormancy during the dry or summer season.*

eunotosaur *Reptile thought to represent first evolutionary stage of turtles, represented by fossil skeletons dating from the Permian era.*

exoskeleton *A rigid external covering for the body in certain animals (e.g., the carapace and plastron of the Chelonia).*

flipper *A broadened limb of a turtle, used for swimming, as in marine turtles.*

hinge *Unfixed joints between the bony plates of the plastron that facilitate movement of the front or rear parts (or of both) for protection of the body shell.*

imbricate *Overlapping like roof shingles, as in reptiles where the posterior end of a scale overlaps the anterior end of that which follows.*

overwintering *Habit of hatchlings of certain tortoise or turtle species that remain inside the egg during the winter until the arrival of warmer weather.*

plastron *Lower or ventral part of the shell of chelonians.*

scutes *Horny laminar formations that cover the bony shell of chelonians.*

sexual dimorphism *Phenomenon whereby, in a particular species, one sex displays morphological or chromatic features different from those of the other.*

terrapin *Common name for various American fresh- or brackish-water turtle species.*

Testudines *Alternative name for the order of Chelonia.*

tortoise *Name commonly applied to define the land species of present-day chelonians.*

turtle *Name commonly applied to define the marine or freshwater species of present-day chelonians.*

Centro Mexicano de la Tortuga
Instituto Nacional de la Pesca,
Mazunte, Tonameca, Oaxaca
Apdo, Postal 16, Puerto Angel,
Oaxaca, C. P. 70902, Mexico.

Chelonian Conservation and
Biology, Journal of the
IUCN/SSC Tortoise and
Freshwater Turtle Specialist
Group and International
Bulletin of Chelonian Research.
Published by Chelonian
Research Foundation, 168
Goodrich Street, Lunenburg,
Massachusetts 01462 USA.

CITS Bulletin
Communauté d'intérêts pour
tortues en Suisse. Metrailler
Sebastien, Rue de la Cure,
CH-1967 Bramois, Switzerland.

Copeia
American Society of
Ichthyologists and
Herpetologists, Business
Office, Department of Zoology,
Southern Illinois University,
Carbondale, Illinois 62901-6501.

Herpetologica
Herpetologists' League,
Secretary: Joseph C. Mitchell,
Department of Biology,
University of Richmond,
Richmond, Virginia 23173 USA.

Journal of Herpetology
Society for the Study of
Amphibians and Reptiles (SSAR),
Treasurer: Douglas Taylor,
Department of Zoology, Miami
University, Oxford, Ohio 45056
USA.

Monitor
Bollettino della Societas
Herpetologica italica, con
sede a Torino, presso il Museo
Regionale di Scienze Naturali,
Via Giolitti 36, 10123 Turin.
Website:
www.unicam.it/socher.

National Turtle and Tortoise
Society
P.O. Box 66935, Phoenix,
Arizona 85082-6935 USA.

Reptiles
Fancy Publications, Inc.,
Reptiles Magazine, P.O. Box
58700, Boulder, Colorado
80322-8700 USA.

Tortoise Trust
BM Tortoise London, WC1N 3XX,
England. Phone: 0044. 1267.
211578. USA, 5667 Snell Avenue,
San José, California, e-mail:
ttrust@phc.net.

Tortuga Gazette
California Turtle and Tortoise
Club, Sales Committee, P.O. Box
7300, Van Nuys, California
91409-7300 USA.

TRAFFIC
Europe Enforcement Project,
Barbaralaan 120, 4834 SM –
P.O. Box 4625, 4803 EP Breda,
The Netherlands, e-mail:
traffeur@antenna.nl.

Inter-American Convention
for the Protection and
Conservation of Sea Turtles.
Website:
http:/www.seaturtle.org/iac.

CITES. Ministero dell'Ambiente,
Servizio Conservazione Natura,
tel. 06/78466210. Corpo
Forestale dello Stato, Servizio
CITES, tel. 06/46657222.

Société Herpétologique de
France, Groupe Cistude, 3 rue
Archimède, F 91420 Morangis,
France, e-mail: emyso@aol.com.

The British Chelonian Group,
c/o Bob Langton, 13 Springfield
Road, Exmouth, Devon, EX8 3JY,
UK. Fax +44 1395. 270720.

253

The author expresses his thanks to:

Christiana Soccini for her invaluable advice and patience in the preparation of the text; my colleague and friend Toni Calmonte for a wealth of personal photographic documentation and information on the ecology of certain species of Chelonia from Mexico and southern China; my friends Guido Tavecchio, Franco Andreon, Marco Cattaneo, Luciano Di Tizio, Livio Emanueli, Jesus Zuniga and Andrea Picco; Pino Bardi and his staff for the ready availability and quality of graphic work; Antonio Busetto for the care with which he prepared the illustrations.

ACKNOWLEDGMENTS

PHOTOGRAPHIC CREDITS

255